A Practical Guide to

Transformative Supervision
for the **Helping Professions**

Amplifying Insight

Nicki Weld

Foreword by Jan Fook

Jessica Kingsley *Publishers*
London and Philadelphia

First published in 2012
by Jessica Kingsley Publishers
116 Pentonville Road
London N1 9JB, UK
and
400 Market Street, Suite 400
Philadelphia, PA 19106, USA

www.jkp.com

Library of Congress Cataloging in Publication Data
Weld, Nicki.
  A practical guide to transformative supervision for the helping professions
: amplifying insight / Nicki Weld ; foreword by Jan Fook.
    p. cm.
  Includes bibliographical references and index.
  ISBN 978-1-84905-254-2 (alk. paper)
  1. Supervision. 2. Transformative learning. 3. Leadership. I. Title.
  HM1253.W45 2011
  361.0068'3--dc22

British Library Cataloguing in Publication Data
A CIP catalogue record for this book is available from the British Library

ISBN 978 1 84905 254 2

Printed and bound in Great Britain

This book is due for return on or before the last date shown below.

To Auntie Qona
(Qona Crawshaw 1916–2009)
who was bold and never gave up

Contents

Foreword

Supervision is becoming of increasing importance in the global environment. Where there is economic pressure to compete for resourcing, and for services to become more efficient, justifiable, and effective, in public terms, there is a corresponding call for more interventionist management practices.

Supervision thus becomes a political site, where the often competing demands for managerial accountability, professional support and development are often played out in interpersonal interactions between supervisors and frontline workers. This micro level of practices is thus increasingly significant in terms of how globally affected policies are enacted and possibly transformed.

It is therefore timely to see a book which addresses the transformative potential of supervision. Weld draws appropriately on contemporary frameworks, such as relational social work and narrative approaches, to weave an approach to supervisory practice which seeks to rise above purely material, technical and bureaucratic motivations for supervision. She manages to carve out an image of supervision that aspires to self and professional development which largely transcends these possibly more transient concerns.

It is a well written work, drawing on a wealth of experience, and disparate but inspiring sources, to provide a picture of supervision which provides learning for both supervisor and supervisee. It will make readers think again about what they are expecting to provide in, take to, and take away from, supervision.

Jan Fook
Director, School of Social Work, Dalhouse University,
Nova Scotia, Canada

Introduction

It is not the end of the physical body that should worry us. Rather, our concern must be to live while we're alive – to release our inner selves from the spiritual death that comes with living behind a façade designed to conform to external definitions of who and what we are.

Elizabeth Kübler-Ross (1926–2004) (1986, p.164)
(used with kind permission of the
Elizabeth Kübler-Ross Foundation)

I have been providing supervision for the past 15 years, mostly within a social work context, and believe that the time has come for supervision to further advance by becoming more dynamic in purpose and function.

Most supervisors are now clear about the purpose of supervision, contracting, how to structure a session, setting an agenda, managing challenge, and working from reflective practice models. In this book, I am interested in exploring how supervision can become more transformative as a way of amplifying insight to contribute to positive professional and personal change. We must approach exploring and applying transformative supervision from the key principles of respect, dignity, kindness, and integrity, and always from the place that what we do as supervisors is in the best interests of the practitioner and ultimately those whom they serve.

First I need to openly name my own philosophical motivation and possible bias behind exploring transformative change as a function of supervision. I see my life purpose as fundamentally about learning to support the development of awareness, knowledge, and self actualisation. As Pierre Teilhard de Chardin expressed in his work *The Phenomenon of Man* (1955, translated into English 1959), human beings are challenged to learn through physical, biological and spiritual processes that increase consciousness. It is through these processes that we truly awaken to our own divinity and embrace our capacity for transformation and contribute to evolution. The key to this is about learning, and I believe that as human beings the place where we most often learn is within relational contexts. It is through our interactions with others that we learn a great deal about ourselves, other people, and the world that we share. If we have chosen to put ourselves directly in the pathway of relational experiences through being in work that is of service to others, then we have a responsibility to be always reflecting and opening ourselves to the learning that this brings. Learning is about ways of enhancing and expanding our analytical and intuitive knowledge base that in turn increases the potential for professional and personal development.

Being prepared to be involved in this type of continuous insightful learning is what enables our true selves to be most evident in everything we do. It is through openness and honesty that we truly connect to others, and supervision, through being a protected relational space, is naturally a part of this. If we embrace supervision as a place of learning we have nothing to fear from it. The possibilities of expansion and self actualisation (being psychologically whole or complete) become an exciting journey that we can engage in to support positive change in ourselves and our world. Marsha Sinetar in her book *Ordinary People as Monks and Mystics* talks about our own growth as containing two co-existing and equally necessary elements: self knowledge (knowing who the self within us really is and awakening to the values, needs and wants of that self), and the ability to act out that real self in our lives (1986, p.14). Our growth is about paying attention, developing awareness, and using this to translate into expanded and enhanced knowledge.

Too many people wander about in this world unrealised and unaware of their true potential. We have messages galore from the day we are born about how we must be in order to fit into society. While it is useful to have rules and structure in a busy over-populated world, when this creates dogma that denies people the opportunity to be their true selves, a stifling and shutting down of potential occurs. Jochen Encke (2008) quoted in Shohet (2008) talks about the need to step outside of 'our self created boxes... stories are like boxes we build around ourselves to give us structure, identity, security and or familiarity' (p.18). We need to recognise when our 'boxes' are no longer serving us well, when they compromise our ability to grow and achieve self actualisation. In our work this is about being prepared to increase our expertise and deepen our understanding about how and why we do what we do. In short, it is about developing our self awareness so we can be more connected and true to the world and ourselves, and if in the area of service to others, bring our very best to this.

If our goal in life is to understand what it means to be human and to learn from life and then give this learning back to the world, then shutting down through required conformity will hinder this. This is the same within professional contexts and is usually evident in people not seeking professional learning experiences that cast them open again to further self development. This is sometimes seen in practitioners being resistant to, or under-utilising supervision. Peter Senge says 'Real learning gets to the heart of what it means to be human. Through learning we become able to do something we never were able to do. Through learning we extend our capacity to create, to be part of the generative process of life. There is within each of us, a deep hunger for this type of learning.' (1990, p.14). Rather than a choice, I see that learning through reflective practice forums such as supervision is an essential obligation to our work.

Describing supervision

Supervision is now an integral part of most organisations that work within the spectrum of social services. Figure 1.1 summarises how I see the process of supervision and how this ultimately contributes to personal practice theory. This draws from Jan Fook's work about critical reflection and how this contributes to developing personal practice theory by practitioners linking their reflections back into formal theoretical frameworks to help build practice theory (Fook, Ryan and Hawkins 2000, p.231;Fook 2009).

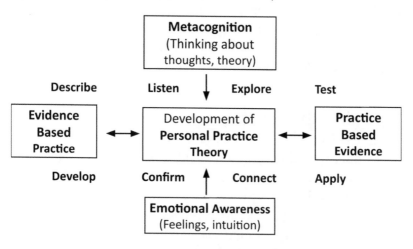

Figure 1.1: Supervision – building personal practice theory

As Figure 1.1 illustrates, there are a number of key information sources that feed into the development of personal practice theory, and are brought to the surface using reflection and questioning. Evidence based practice brings proven techniques, theory, and skills to the supervision session, and supervisors either contribute these or help a practitioner identify and name them for themselves. Practice based evidence or practice wisdom is developed from practice experiences gained by working in a given field, and can also contribute not only to personal practice theory, but also to new evidence based practice ideas through further research and theoretical linkages.

By identifying and drawing on metacognition (thinking about our thinking), and emotional and intuitive awareness, personal practice theory is further enhanced and developed. When connected to practice based evidence and evidence based practice, these types of reasoning are strengthened, challenged and supported. Susan Blumenfield and Irwin Epstein (2001) suggest that intuition and experience need to be fed by empirical information in order to develop the highest quality practice (p.4). It is important that supervision helps practitioners to give voice to emotional knowledge and make evidence based links to intuitive reasoning. I will explore this further in Chapters 4 and 5. The key way to draw on all these information sources is through reflective practice techniques which are applied to help name, discuss, explore, test out, and redevelop ideas and their application.

Expanding the learning potential of supervision

Supervision is often described as a one way street with regard to learning. Discussions have tended to focus on the supervisor supporting and strengthening the supervisee's personal practice theory but with little discussion about what the supervisor has learned in the process. I believe it is impossible to provide effective supervision without learning also occurring for the supervisor. The concept of the 'butterfly effect' goes someway in explaining this for me. The butterfly effect notion derives from chaos theory applied to weather patterns and the concept came from a title of a presentation by Edward Lorenz to the American Association of the Advancement of Science in December 1972 called 'Predictability: Does a butterfly flapping its wings in Brazil set off a tornado in Texas?' It is the idea that small changes in one system may cause larger changes for each iteration, ultimately amplifying what is occurring. Using this theory, each opportunity for learning in supervision has the potential to enhance learning for other people participating in supervision in an ongoing cycle.

I am interested in how this concept might apply to supervision especially through the learning undertaken by a supervisor. By applying the concepts summarised in my supervision process diagram, we can see the mutuality that can exist in a supervision session, which draws on both the supervisee and supervisor's practice wisdom, evidence based practice, metacognition and emotional awareness which are deepened and strengthened through reflective exploration. While the focus is explicitly on developing the supervisee's personal practice theory, the supervisor's is also developing. The processes of describing, listening, exploring, testing, developing, connecting, and applying thoughts, theory, emotions, and intuition are in fact occurring for both the supervisee and supervisor.

So as with the butterfly effect, what the supervisee brings from their experience, creates the potential for change and growth for the supervisor. This knowledge might be carried into another supervision session by the supervisor with someone else and so the ripples of change continue onward. For me this connects back to the fundamental premise of this book – exploring being human and always striving to expand our self learning and contribution to the world we live in. This also gives the lead in supervision to the supervisee, as it is through what they bring that change and development can occur on a multiple of levels. Supervisors are not required to be subject matter experts in every aspect of practice; instead they are required to be skilled in eliciting and supporting other people's reflection, insight, and solution finding capacities. Practitioners with greater experience are less likely to see supervision as a place to be directly taught or given knowledge, but rather a place to explore and develop this through opportunities to consider different perspectives on their actions and practice (Herkt and Hocking 2007).

When we bring stories of practice, dilemmas, and experiences to supervision, we bring the story of us. Andrew Pithouse (1987) suggests 'within their professional worlds human service workers attend to the narratives of others and create/author their own as a part of their everyday work'. One of the social workers at the hospital where I work said that supervision is 'about finding your way through the story to the worker'. As supervisors we engage with a worker who has brought some type of story into the supervision room that they have become a part of. Through listening and working with this narrative, it also becomes part of our story as we join in the process of interpretation and exploration with essentially only ourselves as the tool to do this.

For me, part of embracing supervision as fundamentally a learning experience is recognising that each supervision session I am a part of as a supervisor, teaches me something and I tend to construct a narrative of some sort in relation to it. A Maori concept that captures this well is 'ako' – to learn as well as to teach, where the 'teacher can become the learner, and the learner the teacher' (Royal-Tangaere 1997, pp.50–51, cited in Munford and Sanders 2010, p.8).

Therefore this book, while speaking to us as supervisors in terms of exploring the transformative function in supervision to assist supervisees, also applies to our own learning and self awareness. It assumes mutuality and reciprocity are constantly in action, which I see as also helping reducing the inherent power imbalance that can exist within supervisory relationships. In relation to this, I want to thank those who I supervise and other supervisors I talked with, for their permission to share their experiences and ideas in this book.

Chapter 1 will begin by defining the transformative function of supervision in more depth. We will then explore in the subsequent chapters key factors that enable this function to come alive within supervision. This includes exploring the relational foundation required to support working in this way, the role of observation and questioning, the importance of working with emotions, exploring the role of intuition, and discussing the influence and impacts of the contexts in which supervision is provided. The final chapter explores how supervisors can step up as practice leaders, and identifies further ways to support our own transformative work. It should be noted that the material contained in this book assumes a level of competence in being a supervisor and this is not an introduction to supervision.

We live in a world that requires the best of us. Supervision has been increasingly providing important opportunities for us to learn and develop that support this. It is time now to bring supervision to a new place by building in more of a transformative function so we can continue to ensure we are being all we can be in the complexity of the world that we live in. Change begins with us, and the task of challenging ourselves to transform what needs to improve both around and within us is our responsibility. As supervisors, not only must we too stay continuously alert to being engaged in transformative change, but we need to enable and support it with those whom we supervise. This requires courage, boldness, and leadership, and globally we are at a time where we must step up to this challenge.

Chapter 1

Describing the Transformative Function

Be not the slave of your own past. Plunge into the sublime seas, dive deep and swim far, so you shall come back with self respect, with new power, with an advanced experience that shall explain and overlook the old.

Ralph Waldo Emerson (1803–1882)

So how does the idea of transformative change come into supervision and what does it mean? If we identify the traditional tasks or functions of supervision as described in Brigid Proctor's work, we explore the normative function (professional identity, how a worker is doing within the organisation, teams, their professional role), the formative function (how a worker is in their one to one work with individuals and families), and the supportive function (how is the worker doing in themselves) (O'Donoghue 1998). To these three, we can add the transformative function, which enables a worker to engage in personal and professional change. This is where I see fundamental shifts occur that benefit us as individuals, the people we work for, our professions, our teams, our organisations, and wider society. Transformative work takes reflective practice to a place of observable action whereby the change that occurs results in a shift of behaviour and thinking moving a person in a new direction. It doesn't just create a pause whereby normal function later resumes, it breaks the normal and creates a fundamental shift in ways of working. This chapter will explore further what is meant by transformative work, the opportunities supervision provides for this to occur and current challenges facing supervision that may prevent this type of work.

Describing transformative work

Transformative work is about building insight primarily into ourselves as a way of progressing our own development for the betterment of the world. It is not about becoming an expert, but about developing the ability to perceive or think differently about something (Bohm 1980). Part of engaging in transformative work is the movement from being a reflective thinker to a critical reflective thinker (or reflexive thinker) who can step back and observe their work thoughtfully and be able to make links and connections to it and other places of knowledge.

Critical reflectors are described by Karran Thorpe (2004) as

> individuals who are active learners, who seek out the why of things, who acknowledge a current set of beliefs and values behind their actions, who critically review assumptions, presuppositions from prior learning and who readily change their positions. They adopt a new perspective regarding a concept or situation, which shows learning. (p.337)

She suggests the key to this is self awareness, which links to higher levels of thinking and analysis. Sheppard (2007) suggests 'the reflexive practitioner shows a high degree of self awareness, role awareness, and awareness of assumptions underlying their practice (Sheppard 2007, p.129). I see one of the main outcomes of transformative work as being an increase in self awareness that contributes to positive change that is of benefit both to the worker but also to their work.

So what does the transformative function in supervision look like and how do we know it has occurred? For me this is linked to moments of amplified insight which contribute to an action of change. Indications that the transformative function is operating include:

1. A deep sense of thoughtfulness that leads to a change or shift in values or beliefs.

2. A new behaviour that is immediately put into action in the workplace.

3. A sense of excitement, passion, and motivation to do something differently following a connection to self 'truth'.

4. A named breakthrough in thinking or a new realisation that is connected to the workplace and self.

5. An expanded view or position in relation to an issue or difficulty that connects to prior learning and expands to future action.

It should be noted that these moments do not need to be dramatic or even immediate. Often the place of deep thoughtfulness takes time to fully connect to behaviour and may be realised at a later stage when the application becomes possible. The person may go away and mull over what has occurred and continue to make connections beyond the supervisory relationship. What is evident is that a shift occurs that leads to a positive forward directed change in thinking, feeling, and/or behaving. This is often about enabling creativity and harnessing a persons' ability to make a difference and to fully realise their potential. Joseph Jaworski talks about engaging in 'inner education to be able to identify with all of humanity… if we can do that, we can literally change the world' (Jaworski 1996, p.82).

In some ways these can be described as moments of truth that provide an opening or way forward in personal and professional development through being engaged in a process of learning. These moments of truth are often supported by another person expressing their observation or perception that resonates strongly with what we know to be true within ourselves. A connection is made that makes sense on an emotional and analytical level and a change in thinking, feeling and behaving occurs. Transformative work requires noticing and realising that compel a person to a new form of action. Our typical way of thinking and doing is interrupted and a new possibility emerges. It can link to creativity and reinforces that we have the capacity to grow and change, and if we have that, then we also have the ability to change the world. As Peter Senge says 'We have the capacity to create the world anew' (2008).

The opportunities within supervision

The more I think about a transformative function being explicitly linked to the supervision context, the more exciting this possibility becomes. Supervision is, within most organisations that require it, mandated by policy and seen as a standard part of work requirements, especially for those whose jobs have human contact as their main focus. Therefore supervision is a sanctioned opportunity, providing protected space within the work environment whereby two individuals can engage in learning through a reflective practice process. Allyson Davys and Liz Beddoe suggest that

> Many professionals do much of their work in crowded, noisy, public, and stressful environments where meaningful dialogue and reflection is impossible. Supervision can at very least allow, albeit briefly, the doors to shut, the noise to be reduced and a quiet space for satisfying professional conversation. (2010, p.87)

Therefore, supervision provides a rare opportunity for us to explore both our work and ourselves, and take our professional and personal development further. It can be a place to simultaneously detach and observe our selves in our work, and to fully engage with that self. Michael Carroll talks about supervision as a way of being rather than just a function. He wonders, 'Is it possible that a supervisory attitude, viewing supervision as a reflective process that allows participants to think deeply and vulnerably about life and values, work and career, relationship and connection, might make an immense difference in how participants live?' (Carroll 2001, p.7). David Owen also supports this saying that 'passionate supervision is more than reflecting about yourself. It is where you can see, meet, and get to know new aspects of yourself' (Shohet

2008, p.51). Self awareness through self analysis increases our consciousness of both observation of difference and place of connection.

To support this, as supervisors we need to be bold and take opportunities to put the transformative function of supervision into action for others and for ourselves. Supervision is a place where people can literally draw breath and have unhurried time to focus on their personal and professional learning, knowing that the organisation has approved of this space and the time associated with it. Bill O'Connell and Caroline Jones suggest that supervision should 'recharge the batteries, stimulate the brain cells and empower the worker' (1997, p.292). In some ways it becomes our professional 'base camp' – a concept talked about by M. Scott Peck regarding relationships (1990, p.179). As a base-camp it is often the place we journey out professionally from, and return to to be revitalised, experience security, and replenish ourselves to be re-energised to go back out into practice. It is a unique opportunity that I believe can be more greatly utilised for more powerful learning than currently. If supervision is understood as a place of learning by both supervisor and supervisee, the potential of it is enormous. We must take full advantage of this organisationally protected space to maximise the learning potential it can provide.

Current challenges

There are three main forces that I see supervision as currently being up against that may affect the possible transformative function of this learning space, and which need to be acknowledged. First, I have seen in some organisations I have worked for that rather than supervision being seen as a way of providing a unique learning opportunity, it has tipped into the territory of managing risk adversity through scrutiny and surveillance, and/or as a means of maintaining organisational status quo. Allyson Davys and Liz Beddoe discuss the 'current preoccupation with quality and how the numerous mechanisms to interrogate professional practice have clearly strengthened the mandate for supervision' but in doing so, 'threaten the integrity of supervision as a worker-centred and a learning-focused activity' (2010, p.81). They comment that supervision has instead become 'process driven and dominated by case management' (2010, p.228). Consequently supervision veers between line management (heavy on oversight) aimed at compliance with procedures and checklists to ensure tasks are done, and safe surface exploration (heavy on preserving the status quo). This type of supervision becomes mundane with a 'must do' rather than 'want to do' energy, and does not take up the learning opportunities that are possible. The investment in the relationship becomes perfunctory, and tends to be corrective rather than transformative.

As a response to economically driven requirements, social service agencies in particular have had to shift to working in business type models that are identified by language such as 'productivity, effective, efficient, and quality assurance' along with the responsibility of ensuring their services and those providing them are competent and accountable (Ministry of Health 2000). Organisations become risk averse as a response to the environments they are a part of; usually economically stressed, with a increased level of surveillance and oversight functions (often placed on the role of the supervisor) as a way to prevent the sometimes unpreventable. It is a fact of life that despite best intentions and safeguards, in organisations such as hospitals, child protection agencies and justice settings, sometimes things do go wrong.

Unfortunately a common response to this is one of increased procedural demands, audits, and rules and expectations of compliance with these. These requirements generally arrive as a message of distrust in the competence of workers and can lead to situations where behaviours in need of support and attention are driven underground for fear of reprisals which could be a threat to career and livelihood. Liz Beddoe (2010) writes 'workers become reliant on risk assessment tools at the expense of reflection, practice becomes reactive and mechanistic rather than reflective and creative' (p.6). I will explore these dynamics further in Chapter 6. The same can happen to supervisors who become overseers of practice and lose the focus of supervision as a learning environment designed to promote development. Instead the process becomes yet another form of line management and surveillance too closely linked to compliance measures, performance appraisals and reviews. This is also not helped if their own supervision is managerial in nature.

This is not what I understand supervision to be, and while line management processes need to occur they should be outside of the supervisory relationship. Within supervision there will still be obligations on behalf of the supervisor to notice if standards of practice are met and possible harm prevented. This helps ensure professional accountability and safety, and practice that is responsible to the people whom the organisation serves. This is different from the supervision becoming solely a process of oversight or an administrative checklist of compliance with organisational procedures. The accountability and responsibility functions of supervision can still operate with the supervisor being mindful of where emphasis is placed, and that learning and self awareness to support personal and professional development are the core aims.

If a supervisee feels that supervision is essentially a line management mechanism to check up on them their openness will be reduced and the opportunities for engaging in transformative work impacted on. Herkt and Hocking (2007) refer to this as 'guarding', where supervisees consciously or unconsciously protect themselves by using cognitive avoidance strategies or physically avoiding supervision by not making time for it (p.28). I strongly advocate that the supervision and line management functions need to be performed by different people, while acknowledging there will be small points of crossover from time to time. I also believe and have experience that this can occur with internal supervision within an agency if there is careful attention paid to possible power imbalances and line managers do not provide a supervisory function to their staff.

The second force that results in supervision becoming a place of status quo conversation is one that keeps learning confined to a safe and quite narrow concept. We have all experienced comfortable supervision relationships where we are largely unchallenged and unchallenging. We bring safe topics that stay within unspoken boundaries of what is acceptable to talk about. Transformative change does not live here, and all that results from status quo supervision is ticking the box to meet requirements of having had supervision, and perhaps a feeling of safety as a result of the lack of challenge in the process, but essentially deeper learning is left outside the door. It certainly does not create possibilities for lasting positive change, which is essentially the aim of transformative work. To move toward transformative work requires courage on both sides; the supervisee must be bold enough to bring items to supervision that take them forward on their personal practice learning journey, and the supervisor courageous enough to enquire in ways that break out of safe questioning.

Another factor that needs to be acknowledged is the nervousness that exists for some professions around the notion of engaging in transformative work within the supervision context. This is largely the fear of somewhere crossing the line between supervision and counselling, or having emotion based conversations. While a legitimate fear with regard to boundaries, it doesn't recognise that transformative work need not look like counselling or indeed therapy. I wonder if this emphasis on a rigid professional boundary between supervision and possible counselling has in fact stifled supervision at times, and driven it more into the territory of running through cases and barely discussing the practitioner and their work.

The possible impact of overly rigid boundaries is discussed by Jane Maidment in relation to worker–client relationships. She quotes Kavanagh who says 'it's been my observation that therapists become so concerned about boundaries, and so adept at therapeutic distance, that the therapeutic relationship never happens' (Kavanagh 2002, p.34). The same can happen within the supervisory relationship with the similar distancing and ultimately lack of relational trust occurring. For some supervisors over emphasis on this particular boundary has almost been an escape clause enabling them actually not to engage in deeper reflective work that connects to change and allowing them to skirt around the outside providing only what I call 'case recite' supervision. Kieran O'Donoghue talks about being 'tuned into' the practitioner, adding that 'knowing the practitioner does not mean turning supervision into therapy. It means knowing "enough" about your colleagues to be attuned to them and their work. In other words it means that you are interested in the practitioner not just as a "human resource" but as a human person' (2003, p.129).

This concern about boundaries may reflect unease regarding talking about feelings and emotions. A physiotherapist said to me in a conversation about supervision 'We don't do that touchy feely stuff – we do the touchy but not the feely!' My experience of not having emotion or intuition based conversations in supervision is often due to a fear or discomfort on behalf of the supervisor that they will become overwhelmed by the supervisee's emotion and not be able to handle it in some way, or that something they are shielding about themselves will be discovered. For the supervisee it is often about being possibly judged or perceived as not coping in some way. If this becomes located and justified by the culture of a profession (such as 'we are about doing not being'), it will create barriers to a deeper exploration of learning through both metacognition and emotional awareness. Allyson Davys and Liz Beddoe write 'A clear task of supervision is to support the practitioner in relation to the emotional demands of the work. Increasingly this is understood as how to assist professionals to manage their use of self in their work' (2010, p.229).

Having a transformative function within supervision seeks to take the level of exploration of the personal and professional self to a new and exciting level, and this does mean being prepared to offer questions to elicit insight or sharing of observation. These remain linked to the professional context but are centred on the worker and who they are. Professional groups who prefer to stay with discussions of techniques and not engage the emotional or wider aspects of a worker's journey may need to explore this further if they wish to bring a transformative function truly alive within the supervision they provide. I will explore ways of working with emotions further in Chapter 4 that may help with this, along with providing suggestions to allow the transformative function to be present within supervision and mitigate against some of the challenges described.

Conclusion

Joseph Jaworski talks about one of our responsibilities in life as 'to be open and learn, thereby becoming more capable of sensing and actualising emerging new realities' (1996, p.148). He talks about 'taking a stand and making a declaration to create a new reality' (p.178). I see supervision as a protected learning environment that needs to fully embrace opportunities for transformative change both on an individual and social collective level. As our world struggles to survive we must take any opportunity to develop ourselves in order to support positive social change. As supervisors we need to strongly advocate and protect supervision from becoming a line management surveillance process and preserve it as a learning environment. We need to model willingness to work emotionally and to challenge professional cultures or attitudes that may deny this. Through this we can provide the type of relational foundation necessary to support supervision having a transformative function. This type of supervisory relationship begins from a place of openness and the next chapter will explore this in more depth.

Chapter 2

The Importance of Openness

No problem can be solved from the same level of consciousness that created it.

Albert Einstein (1879–1955)

As supervisors we are the main tool in supervision. How we act, behave, the value we place on supervision and our own congruency within the supervisory relationship will influence the supervision we provide. Central to this is being open – open minded, open to possibility, and open to having ideas and to getting it wrong – as a way to also support workers to be open with us and with themselves. This chapter will explore the key relational traits that support openness as a way to engage in and enable others to participate in transformative work. It begins with discussing the importance of the supervisory relationship and being fully present in this. It then identifies ways to support professional disclosure through our use of self, and the importance of honesty and humour.

The supervisory relationship – being present

Everything in the world is in some way linked through the notion of interdependence, and at the heart of this is some type of relationship. I see supervision as essentially being about a relationship where personal and professional attributes of the supervisor work in connection with those of the supervisee, to enable effective supervision to occur. This point is highlighted by Allyson Davys and Liz Beddoe who write about how the quality of the relationship between the supervisor and the practitioner has been identified as 'the most powerful determinant of the success or quality of the subsequent supervision relationship' (2010, p.50). The importance of this relationship may also influence how a worker perceives the organisation they work in and other relationships they have there. The American Occupational Therapy Association (AOTA) defines supervision as '...a mutual undertaking between the supervisor and the supervisee that fosters growth and development; assures appropriate utilisation of training and potential; encourages creativity and innovation; and provides guidance, support, encouragement and respect while working toward a goal' (AOTA 1999, p.592). This emphasises the notion of partnership that should be inherent in supervision along with the possibilities it can provide by the use of the words 'creativity and innovation'.

The key to being able to include the transformative function within supervision will hinge on the nature of the supervisory relationship. Falendar and Shafranske in their book *Clinical Supervision, A Competency Based Approach* again discuss how the supervisory alliance is, to a great extent, the result of the nature and quality of the relationship that is formed between supervisee and supervisor (2004). They cite Carifio and Hess (1987) who suggest that the ideal characteristics of a psychotherapist may also apply to an ideal supervisor including: empathy, respect, genuineness, concreteness and self disclosure along with self knowledge (Falendar and Shafranske 2004, p.37). Allyson Davys (2005) suggests that valued characteristics of supervisors include having existing competence and knowledge as practitioners, the ability to challenge, competence and training in supervision, and being able to provide support and containment for a range of situations and emotions. They can manage power and authority and are open to feedback and can be self monitoring (Davys 2005, p.16 cited in Davys and Beddoe 2010, p.52).

These traits and characteristics support the notion of openness based on trust and honesty, which should form the relational foundation for supervision. Liz Beddoe writes about the role of supervision in 'preserving practitioner confidence in the face of uncertainty, conflict, and competing interests, and that trust is essential for this type of supervision to flourish and survive... highly experienced supervisors are able to listen, probe and critically question while retaining respect and care as conditions of trust' (2010, p.15).

Developing trust requires getting to know each other and relies on an exchange of information and responses to support it. It requires a deep commitment to get to understand someone, to listen, to observe, to check out, to share, and to give of ourselves. In this way it is not really different from developing any other new relationship except its basis is the professional world and its purpose already defined. It is about building a working alliance based on an agreed working partnership to support professional and personal development and to achieve specified goals.

The care we take in our interactions with another person is essential to providing a strong working alliance. As a New Zealander, a great deal of my learning about showing care and working holistically has been influenced by Te Ao Māori (the Maori world). Robyn Munford and Jackie Sanders describe the Maori concepts of mana (respect), wairuatanga (spirituality), whānautanga (family and relational connections) and manaakitanga (intentional respectful processes and care for others) as influencing and underpinning social work practice that works from a relational foundation (2010, pp.2–11). These also work as key principles within a supervision relationship. Welcoming, taking time, noticing what needs to be attended to, providing care and support, finishing well, and overall considering the supervisee as a holistic being with physical, spiritual, emotional, and relational aspects is essential to supporting relational trust (Durie 1998).

A theory that also captures the process of enabling relational connection in supervision is the 'U' movement developed by C. Otto Scharmer, and described in the book *Presence* (Senge *et al.* 2005). Through the concepts of sensing, presencing, and realising, the U movement highlights processes of letting go and letting come which then carry forward into moving into action and trying out the new learning and discoveries (pp.88 and 219, Senge *et al.*

2005). The U theory of movement is something I find extremely helpful in my supervision, both as a supervisor and a supervisee, particularly because of its focus on being both self and other aware which helps builds relational trust.

Applying the concepts of the U theory requires a slowing down and engagement in a process of coming into the room and paying attention on an emotional, mental, physical and spiritual level to what I want to bring and to what may be being brought. In the role of supervisor, the concept of sensing requires me to place myself in a mental and emotional space of directing my focus completely toward the supervisee. I make a conscious decision to give them my attention, and by letting go of what ever else might be happening for me at that time, I aspire to arrive in an open state so they too can be open and together we can journey down the 'U' to be fully present – to let go and to let come.

This also requires me to project calmness; many times people arrive in supervision having come straight from a busy work context. This includes us, as supervisors, too. The last thing a busy worker needs is a supervisor exuding their own degree of stress. I find stopping my own work at least 15 minutes before I enter the supervision session, getting a hot drink, leaving my cell phone behind, picturing and thinking about the person so they begin to be in my mind, reading over the last session notes, all help with me fully arriving in the room. I see this almost as an image of a rock in busy stream – steady, unfazed, present and stable. I also need to remain passionate and enthused by my work as having supervision with someone who appears jaded or 'over it' in their own work space drains energy from a supervision session. It also does not model congruency if we are trying to help people remain passionate about their work while not feeling this about our own work and/or in our supervisor role.

In realtion to this, Joseph Jaworski quotes a conversation he had with Francisco Varela (a professor of cognitive science and epistemology) who said 'when we are in touch with our "open mind", our emptiness, we exert an enormous attraction to other human beings...there is great magnetism in that state which has been called by Trungpa the "authentic presence'" (Jaworski 1996, p.179). I think this is very true. As human beings we are highly sensitive to nonverbal cues as these are often better predictors of danger than verbal ones. Much of our communication is nonverbal so it makes sense that someone who is in a state of openness is more likely to provide a context and environment for others to also be more open. The sense of someone who is not only paying you attention but is also sending a message of openness is way more conducive to sharing and learning, than being with someone who appears distracted and defended. Jospeh Jaworski talks about becoming an 'open system', through listening, absorbing, asking questions and building understanding (1996, p.152).Very simply openness provides a pathway for greater connection.

Eckhart Tolle's work on the 'power of now' also complements this notion of 'presencing' whereby the focus is on what is happening right now in the room, and requires especially the supervisor to be present and alert to the moment (Tolle 1999). This means noticing thoughts that take away or distract from the present moment and bringing oneself back to being in the now with the practitioner. This is an interesting challenge in a supervision session because supervisors are managing both the content of what has been brought, and facilitating the space that it is being shared within. This sometimes requires thinking forward to what might need to be covered or concluded within the designated time, along with developing questions to assist the reflective process. For me the easiest way to stay in the now and remain present is to focus my attention on the supervisee's words, body language and reactions. This can be described as 'mindfulness' or the process of being fully aware, conscious, and attentive to what is happening in the present moment. It is a process of heightening my powers of observation to remain utterly with the person and to stop myself second guessing or feeling the need to have an answer at the ready. We always know when someone is fully present and giving us their attention, and it is one of the most important relational gifts we can provide.

Supporting professional disclosure and the importance of empathy

To support a foundation of openness, trust, genuineness, and honesty, as supervisors we must mirror this in all that we bring to the supervision session. Ultimately supervision is about professional disclosure and for this is to occur I too need to consider ways to mirror it. This includes ongoing consideration of my own professional self disclosure in a way that is focused on bringing benefit to the supervisee and at the same time sends a message that is ok to table mistakes, worries, and successes. This embraces the notion of 'story telling' through the sharing of wisdom and experience. The sharing of stories can be how we communicate, while always staying present and alert to our motivation for doing so.

By taking care to connect to the context of what is being shared, locating an experience where I too may have struggled, can help with supporting and normalising an experience for a practitioner. It is important to first check if it is ok to share a description of my experience, keep it relatively brief, and end with a question such as 'I'm wondering if that may have happened for you?' which relocates the focus back to the supervisee and their story. This can be very constructive as long as it doesn't become a rambling on about me, or an ego story about how well I did something! For me one of the aims of using personal and professional self disclosure as a supervisor within supervision is to provide permission for someone else to express vulnerability, and also to reinforce an inherent human connection which provides for greater openness. Relevant professional and personal disclosure on the part of the supervisor also supports the process of mutuality and reciprocity whereby there is a giving back or 'gifting back' which can help address some of the power imbalances that naturally exist in supervision (Maidment 2006, p.119).

Another key to openness is being in a place of empathy throughout the supervision session. Empathy based supervision requires the supervisor to stay alert to and tuned to the experience and reality of the supervisee. It is about suspending our mental chat and locating to what is occurring for the other person. For me empathy is fundamentally about 'seeing' another person – and it is therefore the foundation to all supervision. With empathy present and evident in what I ask and what I offer, the supervision session does not slip off into a focus on me, but enables me to remain alert to the person I am with. Put simply empathy says 'I see you' (Weld 2009, p.15).

Having empathy as a key factor in the supervision relationship also allows for greater awareness of some of the possible issues of professional disclosure for the supervisee. To go into a room with someone who may hold greater experience, or perceived status than yourself, and freely talk about possible mistakes you have made in your work is no easy feat. Allyson Davys and Liz Beddoe (2010) identify barriers to self disclosure that include fears about being attacked or criticised, a lack of sensitivity, crossing into counselling, a lack of confidentiality including information being used in disciplinary processes, and a degree of interrogation entering the supervision relationship. On a similar note in relation to difficulties around professional disclosure, Michael Carroll talks about supervisees who have a sense of shame, have difficulty reflecting and learning, are not necessary emotionally aware, struggle to move from theoretical constructs, and tend to seek what is familiar. (Carroll 2006, 2009). As supervisors we do not necessarily recognise or name these barriers enough. The fear of judgement tends to be strong in most of us and it is usually only those who feel very competent and confident in their work who will not struggle to table a mistake or an error of judgement. A physiotherapist at Wellington Hospital suggested this is probably because this type of practitioner has a strong enough practice foundation and professional identity to be able to withstand scrutiny of a possible mistake or identified point of missing knowledge.

The best strategy to manage fears around professional disclosure is again to strive for a nonjudgemental approach toward the supervisee through an environment of openness and an appreciation that mistakes are often key learning opportunities. The strengths based practice principle (St Luke's Innovative Resources Centre, Bendigo, Australia) of 'The problem is the problem not the person' is a helpful philosophical place to operate from in supervision. In this way we can separate people from their behaviour and examine where it may have come from and what might need to be different next time. This enables supervision to again be a partnership that comes from a place of respect and willingness to work together to continuously add to building personal practice theory. Empathy, compassion, acceptance and a solution focused approach (developed primarily by the founders of the Brief Therapy Training Centre, Steve de Shazer (1988) and Insoo Kim Berg) that helps move into a place of future action all support professional self disclosure, along with a willingness of the supervisor to also share relevant experiences.

The role of 'honest honesty' and humour

Another way to build trust so openness can occur requires what I see as modelling and showing 'honest honesty'. I have sometimes come away from supervising with a nagging awareness that I didn't seize a moment to be honestly honest about an observation or wondering I had, and consequently lost the moment and reduced the possibility of engaging the function of transformative change. I have taken part in numerous supervision contracts where 'being challenged' is named as something the supervisee wants (usually said with a slight degree of trepidation it must be noted!), yet I wonder how often we do really name and challenge in supervision. By 'honest honesty' I mean owning my observation, perceptions and beliefs as my own but being prepared to go fully into the dialogue when I see something that may need to change. My friend Mandy O'Neill talks about this as 'being with what it is' (personal communication), that it is about naming what you observe is happening right in the moment in the supervision session. Instead of honest honesty sometimes I have noticed myself skirting to the side of 'soft honesty', which almost talks itself out of the picture by practically apologising for being named!

I had a fantastic experience of honest honesty in my own supervision when I was talking more and more excitedly about how vehemently I didn't agree with a colleague around a very value laden issue. My supervisor quietly let me rave on, venting my emotional upset, and I became more and more justified in my own values on the topic. Then when there was a pause in my stream of consciousness, she leant forward just slightly, made direct eye contact with me and said 'Nicki, be careful that in managing this issue you too don't go to the other extreme of the argument and join with this person through also developing a fundamentalist position.' Her comment stopped me in my tracks and made me instantly reflect that yes, in fact I was heading toward a smug satisfied place of self righteousness, which was the exact behaviour I had found myself up against. It caused me to consider and stay aware of when I too might head toward a counterview that would also be a fundamentalist position.

My supervisor could have tiptoed around this; she could have colluded with me about how terrible it all was and we could have discussed some strategies, but instead what she did was set up a transformative moment for me. While remaining empathetic and supportive of the obvious emotional impact I had experienced, she named with absolute honest honesty that arrived as totally respectful (no flinching, avoiding or dodging), the exact issue I needed to take care about within my response to my colleague. In doing this she also helped me to be aware that I couldn't race off and change another person but I could change my reaction. Through this she helped me come to a more logical and productive response.

I recognise the above example as a transformative moment because first it provided insight, second it shifted my thinking and position, and third I did something different as a result of it. You can see that in terms of what my supervisor did, nothing wildly exceptional happened. She didn't produce an astonishing piece of knowledge or use a radical technique, she relied on the openness that we have in our supervisory relationship, applied her awareness of me, named 'what is' and was simply very honest.

Openness also occurs by us sharing what we notice, appreciate, and enjoy. It is important we take the time to share an observation that goes beyond benign statements such as 'good work' to 'I really liked the way you did…what I saw in that is…well done'. These types of statements are more likely to elicit openness as they send a message that we are really seeing and recognising the person in front of us as a unique and special human being doing what they can to do good work. We can also invite workers to tell us what they thought they did well or ok in their work as frames for positive experiences from their perspective, and we become the listeners and affirmers of this. This again encourages mutuality where we are not sitting in the position of expert and are instead enquirers of practice. Self realisation is a key to transformative practice.

Last, humour is an essential component of supervision to help support openness and increase warmth and positive interaction in the supervisory relationship. Humour is a great ice breaker at the beginning of a supervision session to help a supervisee relax into the session, and brings a sense of both being human as well as working professionals. Used carefully it can help people let go of stress and supports a sense of resilience. As my mother (having now survived two major earthquakes in Christchurch) says, 'Sometimes you just have to find something to laugh about to help you keep going'. For me humour has often been a key factor to help build and sustain positive supervisory relationships, it can be a powerful healer and provides a valuable way to enable human connection.

Conclusion

By ensuring openness is the relational foundation within supervision, we have set the scene for the transformative function to come alive. Alongside this, if we want supervisees to connect with the learning and transformative opportunities supervision can offer, we must bring empathy, honesty, humour, passion, attentiveness, self disclosure, excitement about learning, presence, and commitment to the process. We need to stay mindful of barriers to professional self disclosure and conscious of helping reduce these. Communicating an interest in the person and enjoyment in the whole process of their learning and exploration is fundamental to helping others engage in a learning journey. From here the next step is how we further communicate our observations in order to help transformative moments to arise.

Chapter 3

Applying Our Observations

There are only two ways to live your life; one is as though nothing is a miracle, the other is as though everything is a miracle.

Albert Einstein (1879–1955)

Just about everything we do, think, and feel begins with an observation. Observing allows us to slow down, bring into focus, look, see, and notice what is happening before us. In supervision the key tool that the supervisor brings is observation of the supervisee's story, mood, words, actions, thoughts, feelings, values, beliefs and views. The supervisor observes, notices their observations then offers them out in the form of a statement or question, or through the sharing of relevant information or knowledge. The key to observations in supervision is that they remain centred and connected to the supervisee and the issues they have raised. This chapter will look at how we can deepen our observations to contribute to transformative moments in supervision. It will look at two approaches that can be applied, then describe ten techniques and skills which will continue to be added to over the following chapters.

The personal self

To bring the transformative function alive in supervision requires a subtle shift in the way our observations are shared and applied. The first shift is about bringing more of the personal into the discussions of the professional. This doesn't mean engaging in therapy or crossing a boundary into counselling, but simply applying more of our knowledge of the practitioner into the observations that we share with them. Transformative change occurs when people make a connection to a new idea, thought, behaviour, or approach, and a powerful way for a supervisor to enable this, is to make an explicit connection to the person who sits behind the professional work. This requires the notion of 'tuning in' as discussed in the previous chapter (O'Donoghue 2003). When we tune into the person before us, we are interested in them as both practitioners and human beings.

In my co-authored book *Walking in People's Worlds* (Weld and Appleton 2008) we talked about 'minding the gap between the personal and professional selves' (pp.6–15) using the argument that if people do not bring a congruence of these two selves to their work they will either arrive as very clinical (limited personal self present) or too unstructured and lacking in professional boundaries (limited professional self present). Ruch *et al.* (2010) talk about social work novices who soon discover that too much personal self disclosure may weaken their perceived authority, while too little meant they might be perceived as remote or disinterested, hence less likely to establish working rapport (2010, p.47). If we are especially engaged in work directly with other people, a congruence of these two selves is essential.

I notice working in health, that people often want a connection to a human being, not just a mechanistic approach that results in them feeling devalued and not seen as a person in their own right – a medical condition to be fixed. They also need reassurance that the person caring for them is trained, does have knowledge and skills, and will do a good job. If I hold a belief that integration of the professional and personal selves is key to doing great work, then as a supervisor I must also take the time to ensure I notice and speak to both selves within the supervision context. This requires getting to know the person you are supervising, not just as a practitioner but as a human being. As some workers will be in environments that may feel depersonalising through high levels of administrative systems and audit demands, it is essential we don't carry this depersonalising into supervision. Bringing more personal self observations located back to that of the professional self supports supervisors to make a more meaningful connection with workers and open up the possibility of transformative change.

So how do we do this so that it doesn't feel like we are heading off into the realm of counselling or therapy? I find using language such as 'Something I've wondered about your work is…have I got this right?' 'Can I tell you something I'm noticing in what you have described?' is respectful, linked to the work context, and given most human beings are naturally curious about how they are perceived, also likely to get someone's attention! This type of appreciative enquiry and collaborative approach also allows for the person to say if you have got it wrong, which may be the case, but in speaking back to this, the focus is unmistakably on them in their work. Begin to include the personal self by the use of their name (but don't over do it) or 'you', state your observation, and then link this back to the work or professional issue that is being tabled.

An example of this was shared with me by a supervisor who had a good relationship of openness and honesty built with her supervisee over a year. This had given her an understanding of the supervisee and some of her personal as well as professional reactions to situations. On this occasion, the supervisee sought on the spot supervision for a concern she had about an elderly person who was possibly experiencing neglect. She was quite fired up about what she saw as a failure of care and was heading down a track of instigating legal action. The supervisor however, had noticed in the past that this worker did sometimes move quite quickly to a 'fight' or confrontational response as a way of managing her anxiety in difficult situations. Bearing this in mind, the supervisor listened to the worker's concerns and determined from what was being described that the supervisee did indeed need to slow down in her response and instead seek a medical opinion on the condition in question before taking legal action. She provided sound advice and suggestions about how to proceed with this plan, and then finished with the statement 'Take care that you are not reacting from your own anxiety'.

When the supervisee next came to supervision she said that this comment about reacting from her own anxiety caused her to reflect that sometimes she did jump to a conclusion before she had enough information. For her, this had been a powerful moment of realisation and one she felt would help her slow down and not rush to a reaction in the future. Within this example we see a moment of transformative change, initiated by the supervisor naming an observation and directly stating it to the worker, based on her knowledge of some behaviour in the past. She didn't need to take this any further or engage in a therapeutic exploration about where this type of reaction might have come from, she simply named what she saw and made it a little more personal in her statement by saying 'Take care that you are not reacting from your own anxiety'. This was enough of a jolt for the supervisee to cause a noticing and change to occur. The statement stayed in relation to the work context, yet it brought together the observation of both the professional and personal selves.

Offering the unexpected

Another useful consideration in providing observations to engage the transformative function is to bring in the unexpected. Sometimes in supervision relationships we can get into a comfortable conversation that follows a predictable line of thought. The worst case scenario is actually moving into a place of boredom where you are both watch checking and hoping the hour will soon be over. We are aware of the questions that lead a supervisee through a reflective practice cycle, and this should move to the point that the supervisee naturally does this themselves and we simply facilitate now and then through a pertinent question or comment. However, while the reflective practice cycle may be occurring, this may not necessarily lead to transformative moments resulting in lasting change. It is when as supervisors we offer or bring in an observation that is not expected but still relevant, that we can literally 'interrupt' a way of thinking or being for the supervisee and in this potentially spark a moment of transformative change.

This can occur from listening to what is being shared and then making a connection to a piece of knowledge, idea, information, consideration of language, and then sharing this connection or realisation. This can be very creative especially if we pitch it as naming an untested hypothesis about why or how something might have occurred. Usually this type of sharing will spark from an 'aha' moment for ourselves where we see a possible connection we can bring into the room to further explore with the supervisee. It may of course not resonate with the person, but this shouldn't stop us offering it as it may just move a possible fixed pattern of thought. The key is to ensure that it does have relevance to the possible learning that is being explored.

I had an example of this when a worker I was supervising was considering if she was too careful in her work, a trait that she saw as possibly making her slow and not as productive especially when she compared herself with other social workers. This worker's productivity hadn't been in question and to me her concern was reflective of a tendency to be quite harsh on herself and her performance. As I listened to her I wrote the word 'careful' on the supervision notes I was keeping and when I looked at it it occurred to me that if you looked at the word differently it could be seen as saying 'full care' or 'full of care'. When I saw it like this it really resonated with what I know of this practitioner, who brings a dedication and commitment to her work that sees her giving everyone she works with her full attention and care. So I decided to share what I had observed about the word, essentially to help offer a reframe on something she was interpreting as possibly negative. After I shared my observation I talked about how I saw her being this in her work and how I thought it was a very positive trait. She visibly relaxed and said she hadn't thought of it like that, and it helped her feel affirmed in her work.

By presenting an unexpected yet relevant moment of connection and insight, we provide an opportunity for learning to occur that does shift, strengthen or validate thinking that is already in progress. The idea is to offer a different view or observation on what is being discussed that also may help explain what the supervisee is trying to see. This might be offering a theory from another discipline or context that brings light to what is under discussion. It may help in the development in the worker's own personal practice theory by putting forward another piece of the puzzle that helps join up what they are exploring.

For supervisors this is about being brave enough to offer our observations and ideas even when they might seem a bit left field. It provides an opportunity to share a moment from our own experience or learning, or an immediate observation that helps increase learning and development. My offering of my thoughts on the word 'careful' could have missed the mark altogether but what was key was to ensure it was relevant both personally and professionally to the supervisee. If it comes from this place it is more likely to make sense. It is about providing a different lens rather then simply validating or agreeing. It is about putting forward a gentle challenge or insight that makes another person think or feel differently about something.

Further techniques and questions

So from an observation, we can make a statement, a suggestion, or ask a question to help the supervisee increase their insight into both their professional and personal selves. Coming from the premise of moving a little closer to engaging the personal self with the professional context, and being prepared to bring in something unexpected, here are ten examples of techniques and questions we can use following an observation, that can support a shift in thinking or behaviour, and help highlight the transformative function in supervision:

1. On sharing an observation that brings in more of the personal, take care to allow for stillness and silence and not feel the need to jump in with a response. You can acknowledge you are listening through body language, nodding, eye contact, but reduce talk to allow the supervisee the space to keep connected to the observation, thoughtfulness or reflection they are having and to go deeper with this. When they have

finished share what you noticed or simply thank them for engaging in the reflection that they have had and ask what they have taken from it. This type of allowing stillness is key to 'letting go and letting come' as we saw as part of the U theory in Chapter 2, and assists unconscious thought to become conscious. It also connects to neuroscience theory, which shows that when we experience a learning moment we have an increase in alpha waves and serotonin, so what we call an 'aha' moment is literally a brain 'buzz' (Meg Bond – Professional Supervision Conference 2010). It is important as supervisors that we help enable these learning moments to 'be' yet confirm what has happened so the learning is more likely to be retained.

2. If you observe a supervisee struggling to move into reflection, ask them a question how they found an aspect of the situation (say working with the family) and ask them to respond with just a one word answer. Asking people to find one word to capture their thinking or behaviour, creates a reflective process in itself as it requires the person to carefully consider the experience to best sum it up in one word. From here we can further explore the word they give by saying 'So tell me some more about that?'

3. If you observe a supervisee having difficulty building insight around an interpersonal matter, try using the three chairs exercise. I was taught this by Jane Wexler at the Professional Supervision conference in New Zealand in 2010; it is very helpful for literally shifting perspective on interpersonal issues. In the supervision session always have a third chair available. The supervisor first asks the supervisee if they would like to give this technique a try, and then starts by asking them to say what was happening/happened for them in relation to what is being shared (their thoughts/feelings). The supervisor then asks them to physically shift to the spare chair and to imagine they are now sitting in the other person's shoes (who they have discussed) and asks 'What do you think was/is going on for them, what do you think they may have been thinking

or feeling?' The supervisor then asks the supervisee to move back to their original chair and asks them 'What do you see now?' or 'What are your reflections having sat in both chairs?' 'As a supervisor what advice would you offer to someone also in this position?' (only ask this if they have a supervisory role). From this insight build a strategy or approach to best work with the issue should it arise again.

4. For a worker who you observe is ambivalent or unsure about an issue or making a change, try using the Motivational Interviewing technique of doing the 'costs/benefits analysis' (otherwise known as 'Pros and Cons' or the 'decisional balance' – Miller and Rollnick 2002, p.16). Ask their permission to undertake this type of exploration, and then draw up a quadrant on a sheet of paper as in Table 3.1 and fill it in with the supervisee. See what other links can be made to your existing knowledge of the person while you do this, including patterns of past behaviour. Ask them what they want to do and if it is about engaging in the change, help them to move from 'I could...' language to 'I will...' and 'I'm going to do...' This type of 'change talk' helps reinforce their commitment and motivation to change and moves away from ambivalence (Miller and Moyers 2006).

Table 3.1: Cost/benefits analysis (adapted from Miller and Rollnick 2002)

	Staying the same	Changing
Costs of		
Benefits of		

5. If you observe an issue to be of a more sensitive or personal nature try using the narrative therapy technique (Michael White and David Epston 1990) of externalising the issue, through the use of objects, symbols, sand trays, play dough, or

drawing, to help the supervisee give description to how they might perceive or be managing something. Peter Heath and Eveline Crotty did a great presentation on this at the 2010 New Zealand Supervision Conference, where they talked about using objects and symbols to help people critically reflect on their world. Ask the supervisee to draw what it feels or looks like, or to chose an object (from a box of small objects such as shells, symbolism cards, clay, rocks, small toys) then explore why they chose this and what it represents to them. This promotes insight by again asking someone to name and describe why they have chosen what they did to represent something in a certain way, and examines their relationship to the issue or problem in a different light.

6.   If you observe that the supervisee seems stuck or disempowered about how to work with a situation try using the solution focused technique of identifying exceptions or unique outcomes (developed primarily by the founders of the Brief Therapy Training Centre, Steve de Shazer (1988) and Insoo Kim Berg). Ask the supervisee to identify if they have had a previous experience or are aware of a person that reminds them of what is occurring now. This is very useful if you sense countertransference may be occurring in relation to a person or event. Ask them to be very specific about the thoughts, reactions, and behaviour they noticed themselves engaged in. Ask them what they did in the past that worked in terms of managing the issue or what they would chose to avoid doing from what they previously experienced. Ask them what they can identify to bring forward from this to help in the current situation. Ask them what further learning they may require or what thinking, feeling and behaviour patterns or traps they might like to avoid in the future. Help them name strategies in relation to these. Bill O'Connell and Caroline Jones suggest that the solution focused approach with its emphasis on building a respectful, collaborative relationship and affirmation of the supervisee's competence, is a useful addition to the repertoire of any supervisor (1997, p.292).

7. If you observe that a supervisee is caught in a pervasive belief around an issue, try using cognitive behavioural techniques (developed by Aaron Beck and further by Judith Beck) to help reframe or shift this. Ask the supervisee what value or belief they see sits behind what they are describing. Can they identify where this comes from? Do they see it as still serving them well? Is there a replacement belief or value that might be more helpful? This type of approach is very useful in supporting people to explore what they may have decided is a 'truth' but is actually part of an old script that may cause them upset, difficulty, or limit their potential to grow. The value or belief may be both positive and negative. An example of this could be what is called 'rejection expectancy' whereby early life experiences set up a belief pattern that things go well and then a rejection always occurs. This can set up a defensive way of operating in the world where it becomes easier to behave in a rejecting way to pre-empt this happening again, or 'get in first'. This is ultimately about expecting people to behave in ways that we feel about ourselves. As a supervisor this may get directed at you as a type of countertransference and if it triggers something like this in you also then we have an unhelpful parallel process in action! It is therefore important to have a values/beliefs conversation if you sense this might be occurring, or simply to better understand where your supervisee comes from in relation to core beliefs and values.

8. If you observe a supervisee appears to be stuck on developing a way forward, ask them for their best hope regarding an outcome for the situation. This again engages a solution focused type of approach. Explore what would be different if this best hope was occurring instead. Get them to describe this in very specific detail; what would they be noticing, what would others be noticing, how would they know change was occurring. Now ask what would be the first three steps to help bring this into action. Explore what would be different about how they usually work. Check that they feel confident to give it a go, use scaling questions to explore their confidence

and willingness, and also their capacity (Turnell and Edwards 1999). For example: 'On a scale of 0–10 with 0 being not confident at all and 10 being very confident, how confident and ready do you feel to give that action step a go when you walk out of here today?' If the score is low, then go back to what else they might need to help their confidence increase. This solution focused approach is very helpful if a supervisee is stuck or cannot see a possible way forward as it opens up a future picture. Linking this to transformative change is done through them trying something different as a result of this exploration, supporting them to do so, and talking about it further when they do give it a go as a way of affirming and noticing change.

9. If you observe that a supervisory relationship appears to becoming comfortable and less challenging, begin a new year of supervising by having the worker name their personal and professional goals for the year. Then ask how they would like supervision to help support these goals and how we can best work together to achieve them. This helps create a mandate for transformative change, and can provide us as supervisors with the opportunity to make relevant observations and connections, seek places of expansion, and provide constructive challenge.

10. Always name and own our observations. As supervisors we can't read people's minds and we may well miss the target when we apply an observation. However, even if an observation and enquiry is perhaps not a hundred per cent accurate, it may just trigger an exploration to occur. I said earlier in this book, this work is brave, it steps us and those we work with into new territory and moves outside the comfortable supervision box we may be in. If we come from a place of good intent that is respectful and focused, it is unlikely people will resent us for this. In all of the techniques and ideas offered so far, be transparent about what you are doing, and why. Start with 'I'd like to try something, here's what is, would that be ok?' Or 'I keep wondering about something when I'm with

you, can I put it out on the table?' It may make for a degree of nervousness, but real change never comes from us being entirely comfortable!

As can be seen, a number of these ways of applying our observations derive from counselling models and associated techniques. It should be noted that it is only the application of a technique, rather than a full therapeutic process, that is been undertaken. I have woven these types of techniques into my supervisory practice because they make a great deal of sense, and are very useful for everyday situations. Having trained in social work, counselling, and supervision, I am very clear that by doing this I am not engaging in full counselling or therapy as that looks quite different both in structure and content. I use these techniques to enable insight related to the work context. If I sense that a worker could benefit from having a more therapeutic intervention (if they are stuck or continuously falling into a pattern of particular behaviour) I might suggest this to them or assist them to come to this realisation.

The techniques I have suggested to apply to our observations are practical, useful, and well tested, and we should not be afraid to give them a go in the supervision context. Our responsibility is to use them wisely and transparently. Usually what holds people back from trying these types of techniques is a lack of confidence. I find the best way to overcome this is by using the concept of partnership where I name what I want to try and I own when I haven't done it before. That way we try it out together, which also celebrates the place of learning within supervision and the reciprocal nature of this process.

Conclusion

How we apply our observations in supervision, and help people make connections from these that support transformative change, relies on us using an approach that brings forward more of the personal self. It includes taking a risk to offer unexpected yet relevant ideas, hypotheses and pieces of knowledge, and finally applying a range of techniques that help with developing, insight, reflection, and connection to lead to positive change. Guest and Beutler 1988 believe that the best supervisors cultivate in a supervisee a sense of accomplishment, imagination, respect, inner harmony and wisdom. If we too come from this place as supervisors, at the minimum we will do no harm, and potentially we provide opportunities for transformative work to occur. The key is to always stay worker centred and to be clear in our own minds that what we are about to try is in their best interests as we understand them. The next key area for supporting the transformative function in supervision is through the emotional exploration as a means of amplifying insight and professional development.

Chapter 4

Working with Emotion

All our knowledge proceeds from what we feel.

Leonardo da Vinci (1452–1519)

It is critical that we explore the emotional reactions of those who we supervise. The reasons for this are threefold: first if we are engaged in work with other people we will encounter both their emotions and our own. Sometimes these will be positive, other times they may contain fear or distress. Not having the opportunity to safely 'discharge' these emotional responses can lead to professional dangerousness (Morrison 1997; Reder, Duncan and Grey 1993), compassion fatigue, burn out and even depression. Second, if we are working in contact with the emotions of others (or especially if your work is directly with emotions), we owe it to them and ourselves that we are as emotionally intelligent as we can be, so our service is self aware and sound. Third, working 'emotionally' with a supervisee provides rich opportunities for transformative moments, as emotions are often a key source of information about both behaviour and thought. This chapter will explore further the importance of emotions, describe a simple emotional intelligence framework, and will link this to David Kolb's experiential learning cycle, including offering a series of questions that can be applied in supervision. It will then discuss further the supervisor's role to work with emotions to help provide quality reasoning.

The importance of exploring emotions in supervision

In regard to the importance of undertaking what I call 'emotionally aware' supervision Gray, Field and Brown (2010) write

> An endangered species in this pressured supervisory climate can be the management of emotion... if the emotion of our work is not managed there can be considerable impact on our effectiveness. We don't work well if we are frightened, depressed, grieving or frozen. Expression of negative emotion is crucial in allowing people to come to terms with a situation and move on from it...supervision must be a place where emotions can be expressed and explored. (p.53)

As suggested in Chapter 1, one of the possible reasons we don't do this as supervisors is a fear of being overwhelmed or not being able to manage what might come forward. If this is our fear we need to take responsibility to develop ways to better manage it. Simply not going there can leave people adrift and impaired in their ability to work and function. If it is our supervisee's fear and is linked to discomfort around professional self disclosure, we need to provide an environment of openness as discussed, and model this type of expression through sharing our own emotional responses in an appropriate way.

Tony Morrison in his article on emotional intelligence in social work (2007) highlighted this further through this observation:

> Benner's analysis of critical incident reviews with experienced nurses identified that, in acute medical or care situations, the expert nurse had a level of anticipatory, observational, analytical and inter personal care skills that were both care enhancing and frequently life saving. In part, this was achieved by intervening speedily during medical crises, but equally it was by making powerful emotional contact with the patient during such crises that motivated the patient's self healing determination.

> This is borne out by other research in which it was found that cardiac patients nursed by staff with depressed mood had a mortality rate four times higher than expected (Goleman *et al.* 2002). It is clear, then, that the handling of emotion and the process of care are inextricably connected. (Morrison 2007, p.4)

This is a revealing piece of research that reminds us that it is not just what we do in our work but how we are in ourselves that can help or hinder a recovery process for those on the receiving end of our services. If a nurse or any health professional providing care for a person is working from a depressed or low mood they are likely to be protective of the energy they give out. This protective position would be evident in lower levels of engagement and interaction, keeping contact with people shorter and hence potentially not picking up on signals or cues that the person's health was deteriorating. A person may also pick up on the health professionals' low levels of mood and choose not to 'bother' or raise concerns that they could be having, again leaving a potentially life threatening symptom unchecked. I wonder if these very real consequences of working with other people from lower places of energy and emotional availability, may have contributed to the escalation in mortality rates shown in this research, along with the subtle energy transmission of negative or less hopeful emotion.

Staff who lack what Tony Morrison called 'emotional competence' also prove challenging to manage and work with. He says 'As a mentor for managers and supervisors dealing with difficult staff management situations, it is increasingly apparent that the most troubling and intractable situations exist when performance difficulties occur in the context of staff who lack accurate empathy, self awareness, and self management skills' (Morrison 2007, p.3). He goes on to say that this can result in a 'toxicity' that can spread throughout whole teams. As supervisors this is challenging to work with, and requires a lot of skill and modelling along with active techniques and questioning to support workers to better develop their emotional intelligence and awareness. Howe suggests that emotionally intelligent people use their emotions to improve their reasoning, and typically cooperate and collaborate with others in mutually rewarding relationships (2008, p.14,). Emotional awareness is, then, a fundamental requirement of successful interpersonal relationships.

Being prepared to work with emotion also helps contribute to a quality supervisory relationship. Cherniss and Equatios (1997) describe the best supervision styles as insight orientated, with the supervisor asking questions designed to activate the supervisee to solve problems independently, and in a feelings oriented way, with the supervisor encouraging the supervisee to deal with emotional responses to the clinical process. Smith asked practitioners what responses they would like from an ideal supervisor to whom you took an experience of fear. What participants wanted was their supervisor to make time to 'listen to them without criticism…a capacity to understand, acknowledge and recognise' the experience, followed by 'reflection, non critical exploration, validation, affirmation, and confirmation of the supervisees' and support and action as needed (Smith 2000, p.18, cited in Davys and Beddoe 2010, p.189). Rather than being something for supervisors to be worried about, providing an environment of trust and openness where emotions can be shared, can only be seen as positive.

So why see emotions as such a valuable source of information? I learnt from reading Jill Bolte-Taylor's book *My Stroke of Insight* (2008) that all of the experiences we come into contact with must first pass through the limbic system of our brain before reaching our higher cortex. As the limbic system is also our emotional centre, this means our emotions and feelings tend to be activated before our thoughts. They therefore influence our thinking process so it makes sense that we explore and look at them as they may in fact have determined how we have chosen to think about something.

Tony Morrison suggests that emotions are 'deep level signals about information that demands attention as to whether a situation is to be approached or avoided…the rapid appraisal of such signals conveys the meaning of the situation and is often a trigger for action' (2007, p.255). Eileen Munro in her article 'Improving reasoning in supervision' (2008) refers to Damasio's study of people whose emotional capacity was damaged and how they then struggled with cognitive tasks, suggesting emotions do help us in our thinking and decision making processes (2008, p.4).

Related to this is my belief that our emotions are the voice of our intuition, a concept I will discuss further in the next chapter. They provide connection to body, to mind, and how we relate to others in the world. Emotions give us direction on where to focus our attention, therefore we must give them voice in supervision, to help people process, take their learning, and move forward, and also as a key way of shifting thinking and responding to situations.

Defining Emotional Intelligence (EI)

When talking about working with emotions, we cannot help but talk about the concept of emotional intelligence. Salovey and Mayer, building on the work of E.L. Thorndike, a psychologist in the 1920s who first coined the term 'social intelligence', describe emotional intelligence as 'the ability to monitor one's own and other's feelings and emotions, to discriminate among them, and to use this information to guide one's thinking and action' (1990, p.189). Goleman, in his work on emotional intelligence, challenges society's focus on IQ and suggests that in fact emotional intelligence is more critical to enable the social intelligence required to function and be successful in our interactions with others. We will all remember an especially bright person at school who scored all A's, won academic scholarships, and was never heard of again once they left school, while a student who scored average grades, got on well with people, and showed natural leadership ability, is now running a high profile organisation and contributing to obvious social change in our society.

Daniel Goleman quotes Salovey who adapted Howard Gardner's work into five domains of emotional intelligence around knowing one's emotions, managing emotions, motivating oneself, recognising emotions in others and handling emotions in others. (Goleman 2006, p.43). Building on this, Reuven Bar-on in 2005 described five key social and emotional abilities to help manage environmental demands including self awareness, awareness of others, managing strong emotions and controlling impulses, adapting to change and problem solving, generating positive effect and being self motivated.

Further to this, Goleman describes traits such as self control, persistence, the ability to motivate oneself, self awareness, sensitivity, empathy, intuition, ability to express one's emotions appropriately, and being conscientious, as key to emotional intelligence. Essentially emotional intelligence sits behind social intelligence or the ability to manage social relations well. Goleman quotes John Mayer who describes self awareness as being 'aware of both our mood and our thoughts about our mood' (Goleman 2004, p.47). If supervision has a responsibility to give back to society and to contribute to positive personal, professional, and social change, then helping those we supervise to be continuously operating from an emotionally intelligent perspective can only make for more healthy interactions, relationships, organisations and communities.

For the purposes of this chapter I have chosen to condense the key writing quoted about the domains of emotional intelligence into Figure 4.1 as per my article on emotional intelligence in supervision (Weld 2006). My intention is to make it easier for a supervisor to remember and hold the basic premises of emotional intelligence theory to help guide them on both a personal and professional level in their supervisory work.

In the first task we see the interpersonal and *intra*personal skill of being able to identify our own emotional response and being able to name this, and also being able to recognise that it may be different to someone else's response, along with not assuming that just because we are feeling an emotion that others will be as well. In this task we see self awareness (recognising what is happening for us) and also empathy (recognising what is happening for someone else). Goleman names being able to identify our emotional response as the 'keystone' to emotional intelligence, and talks about people who have a surer sense of how they feel, being better 'pilots' of their lives (Goleman 2006, p.43). If we can't recognise, with a degree of confidence, our emotional responses, it is unlikely that we will do a very good job of recognising someone else's. This includes being able to distinguish one emotion from another such as liking and loving, and formulating predictive rules about feelings such as that anger often gives way to shame, and loss is usually accompanied by sadness (Goleman 2006).

The tasks of Emotional Intelligence:

1. **Perceive/label/distinguish** own and others' emotion – self awareness.

2. **Manage and control** own emotions and impulses.

3. **Marshall** and use own emotional knowledge to aid in judgment.

4. **Develop understanding and relate** to others using emotional knowledge.

5. **Adapt and problem solve** in an emotionally responsive and competent way.

(adapted from Bar-On 2005, Salovey and Mayer 1990, and Goleman 2004)

Figure 4.1: The tasks of emotional intelligence (from Weld 2006)

In the second task we move from recognising to then managing and controlling our own emotions and impulses. This can be seen as the task of emotional regulation and normally develops in childhood. From about age two we learn that overwhelming feelings which tend to lead to a need to tantrum actually do not serve us well, and so we begin the journey of emotional regulation. Throwing a tantrum in the workplace generally doesn't do us any favours. Although we may recognise that we are having a strong anger response to our malfunctioning computer, we have to find ways to manage this, including managing the impulse to toss the non functioning computer out the window. On a more serious note, we can guess that many people in our prison system are there due to poor management of emotions and impulse control. If this is coupled with short term thinking grown out of a constant need to physically and emotionally survive, the results can be disastrous. We hear of work such as anger management, which essentially begins with a person recognising the signs and symptoms of getting angry, then finding ways to manage and control this so it does not cause harm. This also applies to low mood, anxiety, and even elation and joy. Essentially the idea is to manage your emotions so they don't end up managing you (Goleman 2006).

The third task involves using or applying our emotional knowledge to help us in our decision making. This is about using the wisdom that emotions can offer us to help inform what we will do next. An example of this was a social worker I worked with who on this particular day had watched a distressing evidential interview of two young girls talking about the extreme physical abuse they had been subjected to by their father. That afternoon the social worker was due to meet with the father. On watching the tape the worker identified that she felt extremely angry and upset about what she had seen and heard, and recognised she couldn't manage these very powerful emotions in time to see the father. She decided based on this awareness, that it would be best to not see the father that afternoon. Instead she asked her colleague if he would instead. This social worker realised that if she did meet with the father at that time her feelings would cloud her ability to conduct an objective and calm interview with him. While she needed to do some further work on managing her own anger response, her recognition of being impaired to work with this man was an indication of emotional intelligence in action.

The fourth task pertains to bringing forward an empathetic response. By recognising what is happening for us, bringing forward prior emotional experiences to make an empathetic connection, and paying attention to the signals of both our and another's emotions we can build a better understanding of what may be happening for them, which can help us relate and better connect with them. I had an experience of being called to see a mother who was being described as 'hysterical' by ward staff. She had a child who would develop severe respiratory difficulties and require immediate life saving intervention. When this happened the mother would become extremely distressed and unfortunately this only heightened her child's distress making breathing even more difficult.

When I arrived medical staff were working frantically to stabilise the child while the mother was wailing from a corner of the room. A nurse turned to me and said 'Get her out of here!' What I was immediately aware of was an extremely high level of fear and panic in the room that was almost being transmitted between mother and child causing both to be escalating in their distress. It was very difficult not be affected by it but I recognised that also responding to this fear and panic from a place of anger would not help de-escalate the situation. Sometimes in situations where things are out of control, we may use anger to assert control, but this reaction from the nursing staff (while understandable) was not helping this mother and consequently her child. I felt that the anger and frustration being directed to her was only escalating her panic and sense of being out of control. Instead I decided that I needed to mirror calm and control with her. She had slid down a wall and was sitting sobbing on the floor, so I got down on the floor with her, took her hands in mine and asked her to look at me. I held eye contact, and asked her to breathe slowly with me. We did this until she was calmer and was able to quietly step out the room so the staff could continue to treat her child.

Later we talked about what had happened without any blame or shaming, and she recognised that she needed to respond differently when these situations occurred so it didn't escalate to panic for her child leading to an even more compromised health situation. She recognised the need to have counselling to talk through the past trauma and fear she had experienced that had become very compounded, so each time her child became acutely unwell, she was in fact reliving many times. We talked about applying practical grounding techniques to help her stay in control, managing her breathing, and focusing on being as strong as she could for her child. This was a turning point for her, and while still finding her child becoming unwell distressing, she managed future situations admirably.

The fifth task, connected to this empathetic response, is about the ability to adapt and problem solve in an emotionally competent way. This is sometimes about creating 'emotional space' to detach from the emotional experience in order to be able to act. Often in times of crisis we almost shelve our emotional response as we recognise we need to take action to get through what needs to happen. As is evident in the above example, it is often easier to do this when it is not you having the main experience! An example might be when we are involved in a car accident. At that moment we realise that our day has just altered course; we now may be late for an appointment, or a feeling of happiness or anticipation about going on holiday just took a nose dive, and it's potentially an expensive one. If the accident wasn't our fault it is tempting to jump out of the car and direct our anger about our now altered day and changed bank account at the other driver. Ultimately though this doesn't achieve anything, and we know that later our anger may run to shame or regret. Instead it is best to take a few deep breaths and decide that a rational and calm approach is probably a better way to go when interacting with the other person who could be experiencing defensiveness, upset, panic or fear. Not only is the interaction likely to go more smoothly, but we won't feel as bad afterward on top of having a now damaged car!

In this everyday (well hopefully not!) example all five tasks are evident. First working out how we feel, what other emotions this feeling might lead to, and possibly how the other person might be feeling. Second working out how to manage and control our impulses to want to leap out of the car and begin shouting. Third calling on prior experiences to anticipate how the other person might be feeling, and finally applying emotional knowledge to best problem solve the situation and to move forward. It should be noted that emotional intelligence be seen as an aspiration – we may not always achieve it but from this awareness of the impact on us when we don't, emotional intelligence can continue to grow.

Applying EI to reflective practice

The easiest way I have found to apply emotional awareness and intelligence thinking in supervision is to apply it to the Kolb learning cycle (Kolb 1984 adapted by Morrison 1993) which supports reflective practice. I have developed some questions that a supervisor can ask when using the learning cycle, as a way of bringing forward more of an emotions-based conversation, and using emotions to help bring about greater insight. These questions are linked to the four phases of the learning cycle: Experiencing (supervisee names the experience or tells the story), Reflecting (supervisee discusses their thoughts and feelings in relation to what happened), Conceptualising (supervisee thinks about their thinking and this is linked to theory, prior practice knowledge, they make sense of what occurred) and Experimenting (supervisee develops new ideas to try and takes these way into their work). As suggested they can be woven into existing questions, or used in this order:

1. *Experiencing:*

    • 'What emotions were you aware of when you were engaged in this interaction?'

    • 'What would another person have noticed if they had been watching or listening to you?'

    • 'What do you think the other person (in the interaction) may have been experiencing?'

    • 'What is happening for you right now talking about this?'

2. *Reflecting:*

    • 'How did you notice yourself managing or not managing your emotions?'

    • 'Can you see any link between the client's emotional experience and your own?'

    • 'What would you change, if anything, about how you responded emotionally?'

3. *Conceptualising and Experimenting:*

- 'Is there a time you can think of when you responded in a way that you felt was ok and relates to this situation, and what did you do that was different?'

- 'Is there a situation you can think of that would help you build an empathic response to this person and their situation?'

- 'How do you "marshal" your emotions to serve you well in your work?'

(Weld 2006)

These types of questions help bring 'emotional language' into the supervision session, which can be useful for those people less ready or used to talking about their feelings. By being woven into the standard reflective practice process they will become more normalised over time. As exploring emotional content can be sensitive, we can move in and out from the issue at hand, returning to safer topics if need be and then working back to an emotional intelligence question. Or, with a person's permission, asking them the questions in sequence as outlined above can provide a deep and powerful exploration of the issue being discussed.

Ensuring quality reasoning

As we have seen, bringing more emotion centred work into supervision helps provide an opportunity for emotions related to an experience to be safely brought up. This helps them become at an observed level of consciousness, expressed and explored, and fully processed. Through exploring emotional responses we also can help further develop emotional awareness and intelligence to apply to our work. Both of these contribute to an overall process of better reasoning especially in situations of high emotional content such as child protection or palliative care work. By identifying and examining our emotional responses, we can engage our cognitive reasoning processes, and influence our emotions by changing the thinking we may have in relation to a situation.

I had a recent example of this with a worker who had a significant emotional response to how she perceived an action of another staff member. This led to her being extremely upset and reacting in a way that wasn't particularly professional (which just added to how bad she felt!). We spent time working through what had actually happened and where she had gone to in her response around it. While her emotional response did give her some critical information that she needed in order to name and find ways to improve this particular working relationship, it was out of proportion for the actual incident she had experienced. In her mind her interpretation of the event complicated by a difficult dynamic and other historical experiences, led her to jump a few steps to a conclusion that wasn't correct and this in turn further fuelled her emotional response. It is important we recognise our emotions and cognitions are implicitly linked and can trigger each other. Developing pathways of reasoning can help manage this.

Eileen Munro in her article 'Improving reasoning in supervision' (2008) talks about how supervisors have a key role to play in helping workers critique their own reasoning, including checking for biases that may arise from working from our more intuitive capacity that is often 'permeated with emotions'. She discusses how, used with caution, emotions are a valuable source of evidence, and should not be disregarded as unscientific or as 'unwanted noise'. It is important though that supervisors bring a more analytical reasoning to bear on what is shared by the supervisee. The supervisor (because they are not directly affected by the emotions as they are usually not immersed in the experience), can help the supervisee slow down, identify the emotional response, analyse whether the response is fully accurate, and check what other evidence is present to support this.

As supervisors we must apply this same analysis of emotions to ourselves and our work. If we are not are aware of our emotional responses to our work and also those of the individuals we supervise, we too can fall into professionally dangerous and unaware practice. We must take care to use our own supervision and reflective processes to assess our own emotional responses so we can bring a more analytical reasoning to our supervisory role. We should be always aspiring toward emotional intelligence in our role as supervisors but recognise when we may not achieve this and learn from this. As supervisors we are not devoid of emotions and nor should we aim to be. Emotions are far too important a source of information for us to try and leave them out of the picture.

Conclusion

Emotions are a key source of information and deserve a valid place within supervision discussions. Supervisors who feel less than comfortable about engaging in emotional conversations with practitioners need to develop ways to resolve this. Helping ourselves and another person identify emotional responses that may not be fully accurate through helping bring about a logical analysis of the situation can be very insightful and also freeing for times when we may end up at the mercy of an emotional response. In this way the process can be transformative as it shifts a pattern of response that makes for better outcomes both personally and professionally in the future. The knowledge that comes from our emotions is a rich source of learning for us all.

Giving time in supervision to bring forward the emotional voice of an experience helps also model Patrick Casement's 1995 idea of the 'internal supervisor' (Ruch *et al.* 2010, p.62) whereby the skills of reflection and applying emotional intelligence thinking can become a natural way of being. This helps provide both an internal supportive reflective dialogue along with the external reflective dialogue provided through supervision (Ruch *et al.* 2010, p.228). As a professional support and development forum, supervision provides a safe and structured way to learn and experience this. Often located behind our emotional response is an intuitive one and this is the next essential place for exploring transformative change.

Chapter 5

Exploring Intuition

The soul can not think without a picture

Aristotle 384bc–322bc

Intuition is a challenging concept to describe, which reflects the difficulty most people have putting into words what their intuitive response is. People tend to say things like 'I got a really strong gut feeling', 'I walked into the house and the hair stood up on the back of my neck and I just knew something was really wrong'. This lack of empirical evidence has resulted in intuitive responses often being dismissed from legal or medical contexts, with intuition not seen as not scientific or factual. However, as Eileen Munro suggests

> we have two separate methods for processing data in our brains, one analytic and the other intuitive…both are necessary for highest level of reasoning…neither intuitive or analytic reasoning are 'the best' but each has different strengths and weaknesses, and in reality we use both in most reasoning tasks…these both contribute to and develop our 'higher level reasoning'. (Munro 2008, p.3)

As supervisors we need to give attention to articulating this type of reasoning with those we supervise. This chapter will explore what is meant by intuition, how if unexplored it can lead to unrecognised/unacknowledged biases in our thinking, and ways that we can further work with intuition to help increase moments of transformative change in supervision.

Defining intuition – from the brain to the gut

I see intuition as first a neurological function involving rapid sensing of usually nonverbal information that is directly linked to the amygdala. This processes and connects to emotions and memories of nonverbal information to determine whether the sympathetic nervous system via the hypothalamus needs to activate endocrine function to support the body's stress response. It is likely this neurological function was originally part of primitive human survival instincts designed to quickly read nonverbal information and come up with a rapid response to respond to physical danger. Primitive human beings with eyesight not as well developed as other mammals needed to rely on other methods of sensing such as hearing and smell to protect them from danger. Signals of danger were then stored as emotional memories and possibly these processes have been passed down through evolution to help with human survival.

Intuition is usually described as 'pre conscious', which explains people's difficulty initially in articulating it. As it tends to be a response to something perceived as immediately dangerous or worthy of our attention, there isn't enough perceived time to come up with a carefully worded analysed assessment of the situation. Generally the first sign of an intuitive response is via our emotions, which is why I describe emotions as the voice of our intuition. This tends to arrive as a feeling: we feel something about a situation that we then translate into an emotion. It is interesting that people say that they had a gut feeling about something given this appears to be happening in the brain. This could be about a hormonal surge of energy to our large organs or as Eastern philosophy suggests an activation of 'chakras' or energy centres in our body. This is illustrated in this quote by SETA (Society of Eastern Thought and Awareness) from their magazine 'Knowledge of Reality' issue 18:

> ...the 'nabhi' or 'Manipur' chakra...its physical location is at about the level of the navel...physically, it deals with our organs of digestion...psychologically it deals with our sense of satisfaction, and spiritually it deals

both with our 'prosperity', 'generosity' as well as with our 'dharma' or our innate sense of right and wrong...

In relation to this, Daniel Goleman also talks about how

the intuitive signals that guide us come in the form of limbic driven surges for the viscera that Antonio Damasio calls 'somatic markers' – literally gut feelings. The somatic marker is a kind of automatic alarm, typically calling attention to a potential danger from a given course of action. More often than not these markers steer us away from some choice that experience warns us against, though they can also alert us to a golden opportunity. (2006, p.53)

These 'gut feelings' are powerful and greatly influence decisions we make in our lives.

It is fascinating that universally when people talk about having an intuitive response they tend to touch their abdominal area. It could also be that an intuitive response is felt deeply within in us, hence pointing further down toward into the abdominal cavity. It is a wonderful reminder of how our bodies, minds, and spirit are linked. I can recall having the opportunity to work with a group of people on a long term project but the more time I spent with them, the stronger feelings and 'gut' responses I kept on getting to not pursue the project as something wasn't right. Finally the feelings became so 'loud' they caused me to make the decision to pull away from the group. Almost immediately I was flooded with a blissful sense of relief and peace. These people meant me no harm, so where did this powerful reaction come from? To answer that we need to examine the sources of knowledge that informs intuition. Otherwise, without this examination, intuition can be used as a justification that hides a lack of analysis, or as a means to resist incorporating theoretical knowledge and increasing self awareness.

Places of intuitive knowledge

I see there being three places of knowledge that inform intuition in a professional practice context. The first is that already suggested of a more primal, universally human response based on physical survival. Located in our senses and strongly connected to our hormonal stress response, this is knowledge we are born with as human beings and is reflected through our instincts often linked to our need for physical protection. This explains how facial expressions are similar across the world such as happiness and sadness, as these provide a predictable base for us to 'read' and determine what is safe and what isn't in human interactions. This knowledge helps us make rapid fire decisions about information and to act immediately especially if we perceive some type of threat.

We see this primal knowledge in action in babies when they are faced with someone pulling a scary face or loud shouting. Generally they will begin to cry and become upset, sending signals they need to be protected from the object or event that is frightening them. Unfortunately when children live in situations where violence is often present these instincts become so highly developed that children often end up in constant state of arousal and can over react to situations which do not carry a threat. An example is a child who lives in a home containing violence and at school, when a teacher accidentally drops a book, the child flinches and has an increase in their heart rate. Being constantly attuned to danger and having little experience of a safe and secure base leads to short term survival based thinking and often a misinterpretation of behaviour in others (Perry 1997).

As professionals we still hold this more primal survival base of knowledge that does inform our intuitive response. We often scan situations, 'reading' the emotional energy or temperature in the room, and forming quick judgements about this. It makes sense; our instincts are there to protect us physically and psychologically and tell us if it is ok to stay or not stay in a situation, and aid us to decide how we will approach the situation to potentially reduce danger or threat that may be present. While closely linked to body awareness it could be suggested this is also linked to wider human consciousness. It is difficult to describe the concept of what is called spirit, love, energy, or even God, but being in connection with a greater energy than ourselves by being truly present in our self, may also inform this type of primitive or natural intuitive knowledge.

The second place of knowledge I see as forming part of an intuitive response in the workplace context, is to do with our socialisation, personal histories, and the beliefs and values that we have developed from these. This is where we learn what is important, especially in relationships, how we get on with others in the world, and what determines right and wrong. Jerome Wakefield and Judith Baer suggest that 'people have cognitive/representational mental contents including conscious beliefs and desires, sometimes irrational, that motivate and guide their actions' (Wakefield and Baer 2008, p.22). They go on to say that people are shaped in ways they may not be aware of by cultural and family rules and other interpersonal processes that form the context and background for their actions, and provide implicit rules that may be followed without awareness.

These influence our mental models or schema, which help us quickly develop views or judgements on situations in order to prioritise, organise, and manage information. We tend to look for patterns or connections that relate to previous experiences and perceive them through a lens coloured by our socialisation. We are also more likely to seek evidence that confirms our deeply held beliefs, just as we tend to socialise with people who are like us, and support our personal constructs of the world. The idea of personal constructs was developed by George Kelly back in 1955 and is a means by which a person makes sense of, shapes, and controls his or her world (O'Donoghue 2003, p.77). We often look for information that confirms our personal construct of a situation and we need to remember as supervisors that we too will be operating from our own mental models and personal constructs. This doesn't mean these will be negative or unhelpful, but it does mean we need to be self aware and transparent in our observations and own what is our interpretation.

In some ways our values and beliefs become like our personal, moral and ethical code of operating, often closely linked to our self identity, and because of this, we must be able to connect them with more structured ethical frameworks that underpin our chosen professional groups. We are unlikely to work in a profession if we cannot align its ethical framework with our own, at least initially. How I perceive a situation based on my ethical thinking and values and beliefs about it will inform my actions and I am likely to be more convinced of my position on it linked to my actions. Our early socialisation is generally where this knowledge is formed. It is where we learn social and emotional competencies to help us function successfully in the world and where we learn right from wrong. It is also where our psychosocial reality is constructed, supported by often early thoughts and feelings internal to a person and shaped by their interactions (Ruch *et al.* 2010, p.221).

It is important to recognise that this type of 'ethical' knowledge is often built from a place of emotional response, behaviour, and consequent learning. As children we will all be able to recall highly emotive situations where we felt wronged in some way. We may then have chosen to behave in a certain way to 'right' this. My five-year-old nephew had this experience recently when another five-year-old boy put his sunhat in the toilet. My nephew, feeling understandably wronged, got this boy's lunchbox and put that down the toilet. Both got into trouble. What my nephew had to learn was that behaviour of retaliation only gets you in more trouble and that other ways of resolving an issue need to be considered. All very logical as adults but not so when you are five and someone just flushed your sun hat! I hope my nephew builds a value into his ethical knowledge base about how it is not ok to do hurtful things to other people's property and that revenge is not always the best strategy – and also to slow down and not react too quickly when you are hurt about something.

This is hugely valuable area of exploration in supervision that can lead to transformative work as our beliefs and values are often deeply held and we tend to fight to protect them as they form a key part of our identity. This is fine if they serve us well, but sometimes our personal constructs may need further development and examination. They may at times be too closely linked to our ego and be serving an old set of socialisation messages and experiences. Again because they are deeply held, they are quick to rise as a response to a situation – 'That's not right!' we say, absolutely convinced, 'But why isn't it?' asks someone else and we say usually indignantly 'It just isn't!' It can take a while to unpack why we really believe that, as we are usually sure that we are right about it without any self examination. If these views become a pervasive belief system, we tend to apply them uniformly to all situations with little analysis, which may lead to professional dangerousness (Reder, Duncan, and Grey 1993).

The third place of intuitive knowledge in the professional context arrives from our practice experience or wisdom born out of experience of working in our given field. As we become more competent in our work, the ways of doing it become more familiar. Practice wisdom is often developed through linking, connecting knowledge and finding patterns within our work that match with our existing thinking. Malcolm Payne describes this as 'informal practice theory that draws on ideas and experience gained in life and practice. It is applied inductively, that is, the theory derives from particular situations and is generalised to other relevant practice situations, and requires decisions about similarities and differences between situations to decide if the generalisation is relevant' (Payne 2008, p.17). We become less conscious of how we do things as we are more competent at just doing them. We don't have to think a great deal about what we are doing, as we almost automatically operate from the knowledge place that we have built and practised so it becomes 'second nature'.

The most obvious everyday example given of this is driving. We will all remember the painful process of having to master the various tasks of driving and how it seemed it would never become a natural process that we wouldn't have to think so hard about, one action at a time. But one day it does, and it isn't until we try and teach someone else that we are reminded just how many steps and what a complicated cognitive and physical task we have mastered. We just do it and don't really think too much about the physical task of driving until something untoward happens to throw us off – like losing steering or braking power, for example.

Eileen Munro (2008) talks about practice experience becoming part of 'intuitive wisdom'. As professionals start out they tend to operate more from the analytic end of the reasoning continuum but as they gain experience and have their knowledge reinforced this shifts to being more intuitive. In my diagram in the introduction I talked about practice based evidence and suggested this as a source of information for developing personal practice theory. Practice based evidence is the knowledge we have built from practising. It usually begins more from us consciously applying evidence based practice and this always feels a bit bumpy and takes time for it to flow naturally. We build up practice based evidence from doing the work and seeing what does and doesn't work. Eileen Munro emphasises that different profession groups have different levels of knowledge needed to begin working. She notes that social workers 'hopefully have the key skills of being able to engage and relate with others to help gather information, assess, plan and carry out identified interventions. New doctors on the other hand can not just go straight in and do complicated brain surgery' (Munro 2008, p.5). What workers need is to be consciously exploring their practice based evidence and linking this to evidence based practice to best inform personal practice theory which in turn can create new evidence based practice if described and written about. This is best achieved through professional development opportunities, mentoring, and supervision.

Another way of looking at this is through the concept of tacit knowledge. The philosopher and scientist who coined this phrase, Michael Polanyi, said 'We know more than we can tell' (2009, p.4). Sveiby (1997) talks about tacit knowledge as the 'old and well known', the background knowledge, skills, know how, subtle methods, and expertise that inform our practice. It is the knowledge we have acquired through learning by doing and is often implicit in what we do. It often contains skills learnt through observation and is not easily taught. It is more oral than written, so not usually gained from a textbook but from experience. It is found more often in interactive narrative contexts such as group case reviews and supervision. By unpacking and articulating tacit knowledge in an environment such as supervision there unfolds an extremely useful opportunity that not only brings this knowledge closer to the observable surface of practice, but also creates opportunities to pass some of the method behind it on to others. As the supervisor is likely to be supervising others, they could, with permission, share this type of skill and knowledge with them, thus sowing it more widely.

I see these three areas of knowledge (primal, ethical, and practice) linking together to inform our intuitive reasoning in our work. An example of this was when I was called to see a three-month-old baby who had been admitted to hospital with bruising to her face around her cheeks. This bruising to her face was suspected to be non accidental, and my role as a social worker was to try and get further information to ascertain if this was the case. I remember walking into the room and immediately my survival primal knowledge was activated. There was a physically strong looking young man lying casually on one of the beds in the room who didn't say anything when I introduced myself. He just stared inexpressively at me and then back at the baby. Although he looked relaxed he also looked like he could spring across the room, and the casualness almost seemed contrived or rehearsed. The young woman in the room spoke quickly, sat forward with a degree of urgency, appeared physically tense in the way she held her hands, and made little eye contact with me when talking about what had happened. On an instinctive level something felt very wrong; there was no warmth in that room, just tension and something unspoken and secretive. I could feel myself tensing up in response to this. Essentially my immediate primal intuitive response said 'Get out or if you have to stay, keep near the door and be very careful not to aggravate anyone', which is what I did.

The next knowledge area that influenced my intuitive response was from my practice knowledge. I asked how the little girl had gotten the bruising. The explanation given by the young woman was that 'baby knocks her face when she moves her head from side to side in her cot, on the bars of the cot, and she grabs her cheeks and kind of pinches them'. The young man, who I found out was the stepfather, said nothing and just stared at the baby. The explanation felt somewhat desperate in its delivery, and developmentally, calling on my practice knowledge clearly didn't fit with the age of child. My practice knowledge from talking with other parents who were being questioned about possible non accidental injuries told me that this was a lie, probably to protect another adult.

My own ethical knowledge told me that something wrong had happened, small children do not ever deserve to be injured and as adults we must be responsible for managing our frustrations or unmet needs. These are not the responsibility of children, especially ones who cannot protect themselves.

My overall intuitive response to this situation was: 'This was a non accidental injury, she's lying to protect someone, and I bet that guy lying on the bed did it because wow, he has this really aggressive suppressed energy about him.' This intuitive reasoning happened very fast, and needed further investigation and slower, more deliberate, analytic reasoning to make it come from a more rational place of decision making. Talking with the paediatrician was a next step to help strengthen the analytic aspect of it. As it turned out, we were right, and the young man was charged with assault on the little girl who was put under child protective services.

This story unfortunately has a tragic ending. About four months later the paediatrician and I learnt that that the young man had unsupervised access to the child and during this one hour visit, picked her up and smashed her head against the wall and she died from a massive brain injury. I remember standing in the hallway with the paediatrician when he told me the news and us both nearly being in tears about how this could possibly have happened. What it makes me wonder is whether another worker ran with an intuitive response to this man, perhaps informed by a pervasive belief that led to a perception that he had the right to have time with the child and that the unsupervised time was perhaps due to untested trust in him. Were his needs put before the safety of the child? I don't know and can only speculate about what happened to contribute to this tragic outcome.

Checking for bias in intuitive reasoning

Intuitive knowledge, because it is by nature rapid, needs careful scrutiny and the bringing of analytic reasoning to it. Supervision is ideal for this process. It provides a safe forum for the unpacking of the three types of knowledge I have described to enable further analysis and check accuracy. If we have through our own experiences developed a bias or untested value or belief, the objectivity a supervisor can bring to help us examine this is both invaluable and critical. Liz Beddoe writes that moral reasoning and a more nuanced exploration of emotional responses and concerns can strengthen supervision practice (2010, p.10). It also brings more validity to our interpretation of what has occurred. Our brains have evolved to keep us not only physically but also psychologically safe, and our emotions are generally accurate messengers of our intuitive reasoning. However, at times we may be over or under responsive especially if our values and beliefs are involved, and if we have a high emotional response connected to the situation (i.e. feel passionately about something).

This can also lead us to being fixed in an early impression or view of a situation or person, and possibly reluctant to change this. If we form views too quickly and then don't examine them, we often miss out on other key information and experiences. The problem with holding onto a first impression or assessment is that we can ignore additional information or possibilities that may challenge the impression. This can also lead to practice becoming professionally dangerous and inflexible. Dreyfus and Dreyfus (1986) suggest that 'detached deliberation about the validity of decisions will improve decision making'. Supervision can remind us of the importance of staying flexible in our thinking and open to adapting our assessments. We should always apply our sources of knowledge with care and responsibility, as Malcolm Payne says '... use that knowledge and theory in a caring, emotionally intelligent and supportive way with the aim of disentangling the various elements of a complex system and enhancing the resilience both of the people involved and the social and organisational systems they are entwined with' (2008, p.20). As supervisors we need to apply this type of approach with supervisees.

The importance of giving voice to intuition, which is often via our emotional responses, is also reinforced by Davis-Floyd and Arvidson (1997) who say that 'we need to develop a language to talk about these things [intuition] and talk about them well!' (Davis-Floyd and Arvidson 1997, p.192). Eileen Munro writes about how 'intuitive reasoning can be dominant but workers need to take time later to stop and reflect in quieter circumstances' (2008, p.6). She quotes Thiele (2006) as offering the image of seeing our analytic capacity as a 'personal trainer' for intuition, working on it to attain a higher level of rigour. The supervisor can help to be this trainer, assisting reflective learning around the intuitive response, and in turn helping the analytic reasoning of the supervisee come to the fore. This can, in itself, provide for transformative moments as connections are explored and made.

Further application to identify and strengthen intuitive reasoning

The purpose of greater examination of our intuitive reasoning is to develop a stronger base of personal practice theory in our work. By looking more closely at this side of our reasoning we can articulate and have more clarity about the sources of knowledge informing it. So as supervisors how do we do support this? First we must pay attention to the emotions that are in play and explore these using the type of questions suggested in the previous chapter. This will help reach the intuitive thinking behind the emotional response. Here are five suggestions that can support us to do this:

1.   'What is/was your intuition telling you about this?'

   This is a first step in asking someone to focus more deeply and listen to themselves. It is about naming their intuitive response and then further exploring it to build analytic reasoning to support or question it.

2.   'What would a wise woman or man say to you about how to respond to or think about this issue?'

   This is a question that was shared with me from a friend who attends the School of Philosophy in Wellington New Zealand and what I find it does is cause a pause and a consideration of what a sensible, wise and rational approach would look like. What I particularly like about this question is that it connects a person to their internal wise woman or man – the place of wisdom within them, reinforcing that we often have the answer and do not need another person to tell us. This can be very powerful for people and hence contributes to transformative change.

3.   Unpacking an event. When a supervisee talks about an event, issue, or situation, take time to guide them through looking for the messages, the patterns, personal constructs, previous associations and events that link to it.

   This is about slowing down and looking deeply. A good analogy for this is when you go to a river and sit down beside it and look into the water. First you will observe the speed of the water, perhaps some rocks, and perhaps the depth. As you look more closely you might start to observe the light and how it falls on the water and influences the colour of it, how the water moves around a stone or rock so it isn't blocked, you may even see a fish! When you look up from focusing on the river you usually feel more peaceful. This is another way of engaging in transformative work – moving from one current of feeling or response to another that perhaps is gentler and feels more in flow with who we are. It is about observing and noticing to help us grow and develop.

4. 'What are the thoughts, feelings, beliefs, reactions that you didn't name/couldn't name/aren't naming? What is their source (or the core belief) behind them?'

    This is about giving our intuition knowledge further voice. It asks that a person go beyond the often required rhetoric of daily human interaction and say what they really think even if it might be a bit shocking. This relates back to the idea of 'honest honesty' in Chapter 2, and as supervisors we must not sit in judgement of the person with what is shared, simply guide it if necessary, to ensure that it can serve the worker better (if it needs to). I see this as 'shining the light' on what we often keep hidden. This is wonderfully described by Joseph Luft and Harry Ingham in 1955 in their 'Joharri window' tool which suggests that there are things that we know and everyone else knows about us (like our height), things we know but others don't (hidden), things others know that we don't (blind), and things we and others don't know yet (unknown). Working in a transformative way is about bringing the hidden and the blind to light. It is essential to have the type of supervisory relationship discussed in Chapter 2 to support this.

5. Always work from the premise in supervision of: 'Worry more about unquestioned answers, than unanswered questions'.

    This excellent quote came from a participant at a programme held by Peter Senge (Senge *et al.* 2005, p.214). It encapsulates what I referred to in the introduction as dogma, where we go along and do not question and hence preserve the status quo, which may not be serving anyone well, and may also be hindering personal and professional growth. There is also a risk of fundamentalist attitudes here that can lead to polarised attitudes and views. As supervisors we need to look for times when a worker may be accepting their own and others' values, beliefs and methods without question. As I have discussed the challenge around beliefs and values can be a delicate one as people do tend to have an identity connection to their core values and beliefs. The best place to enquire from is one of sensitivity and respectful curiosity. It is then about presenting an alternative view or a different look at something. It is about showing rather than telling. We should always be questioning and enquiring into the answers we receive, as this is at the heart of creativity.

Conclusion

As mentioned in the previous chapters we cannot do this work with those that we supervise without also applying it to ourselves. Everything that has been discussed in relation to intuition comes to bear in our work as supervisors as we too are having intuitive responses all the time to information being shared with us. Throughout a supervision session we need to be paying attention to what our intuition is telling us and be prepared to share this with our supervisee through an offering on the topic or issue at hand, while clearly owning it as our response. Our intuitive take on a situation is very valid as it is likely if we are supervising that we will have an amount of practice knowledge or wisdom that we might rapidly respond from. The slowing down and applying a more analytic approach to our intuitive reasoning, emphasises why it is so important that as supervisors we are having regular supervision which we are prepared to utilise in transformative ways ourselves. However, an observation I have made around this is that as we progress into greater roles of responsibility within an organisation, our own support often reduces and forums such as supervision are less utilised or available. I find this fascinating given we are actually holding more responsibility and therefore should have even greater levels of personal and professional development. This leads us to the next chapter, which explores the environment and organisational context that supervision and workers accessing supervision operate within, and what we as supervisors need to be aware of in relation to this.

Chapter 6

The Environment of Workers

Duty makes us do things well, but love makes us do them beautifully.

Phillips Brooks (1835–1893) American Bishop

So far what we have looked at to assist with the transformative function of supervision has been on the more intra and inter personal levels between the supervisor and supervisee. However, when working in these types of ways we must also consider the environment and context that a worker operates within, and also the wider context where supervision is taking place. Supervision does not occur within a bubble, it always takes place in what Michael Eraut describes as 'socio cultural contexts and situations' (Eraut 2005, p.178) that are the background of where the work occurs. There are a number of environmental influences and systems that impact both positively and negatively on workers, and I have found the best way to explore and stay mindful of these is through applying a simple social ecological framework that considers a person in the context of their immediate and wider environments.

Social ecological thinking considers a number of interconnecting systems that a person interacts with and is influenced by. Malcolm Payne suggests that people both change and are changed by their environment through adaptive processes. Problems tend to arise through maladaptation to environmental impacts and influences (Payne 1997, p.146). This chapter will apply this type of social ecological thinking first exploring the personal and professional characteristics a person may bring to the work context, then the dynamics of teams or services, and the wider organisational culture.

The political and global context that the organisations are a part of will be looked at in more detail in Chapter 7. This chapter will also consider how we can best support workers and ourselves to manage the impacts of the environment we work in by utilising resiliency theory.

Personal and professional characteristics

Especially in social service work we are the main instrument of our work, and with this we bring our previous work experiences (good and bad), our mental models, our hopes, worries and aspirations. We also bring our ways of coping with stress. When working in services with people, we are likely to come into contact with stress as we encounter the uncertainty and anxiety they may be experiencing. As we have seen when looking at working with emotional awareness these can trigger our own reactions especially if we bring a personal history that has set up ways of working to meet ongoing unmet needs. Darcy Siebert highlights some of these as: having had a troubled parent, having experienced emotional abuse, needing approval, being a perfectionist, having difficulty asking for help, and feeling overly responsible for clients (Siebert 2005, p.35). Personal histories of trauma may also be triggered by coming into contact with another person's trauma. He suggests that all of these along with occupational stressors can contribute to possible burnout.

Burnout is usually evident in workers who become apathetic, disillusioned, detached, cynical, and feel ineffective in their work (O'Donoghue 2003). Darcy Siebert also identified that one of the strongest variables related to burnout was the general perception of working in a stressful place (Siebert 2005, p.38). I wonder if perceiving that your work context is stressful can also be a message about team and organisation functioning and expectations, along with those of wider society. It can also be something a worker may believe in and use as a way of perhaps re-directing the cause of their own personal stress or distress.

Many workplaces that provide services to people are stressful at times and there may not be a huge amount we can do to change that except change our ways of responding and thinking about it. Darcy Siebert suggests that perceiving a workplace as stressful creates feelings of burnout, which in turn creates a perception of greater stress from the workplace and on it goes (Siebert 2005, p.38). If however, we also choose to see our work as stressful because this somehow relates to an innate need to be needed or important, then this is something we can change on a mental model or personal construct level. I am curious about the perception of stressful when it is a perception that may meet a strongly held need for belonging through being significant. Seeing our work as stressful may also reflect that we possibly have not found a source of work that is meaningful to us.

We spend significant amounts of our lifetime in or at our work and it is understandable and essential that we will derive a sense of meaning and purpose from it. If we are truly working in an area that speaks to our senses of purpose and meaning in life, we can even say we love our work, or as suggested 'work is love'. People who come from this place rarely talk of being stressed; their enjoyment of doing something they love which allows them to give truly of themselves brings fulfilment and happiness. I wonder if sometimes perceiving our work as stressful may also suggest a disconnect or lack of fit where we constantly feel emotionally and spiritually pulled in the wrong direction and literally become out of sorts or connection with our self – which is always very stressful. Supervision provides a rich opportunity to unpack some of this feeling and perception and to listen for another voice that may sit behind it. I think perception is a fascinating source of exploration in supervision and can lead to transformative change if a person can learn to alter their perception and thinking to more positively contribute to their outlook, especially about their work.

Dynamics of teams and services

The next ecological system we need to examine in terms of staying mindful of the worker in the context of their environment is the team or service that a person is a part of. Teams are often complex because they are made up of individual people and possibly different professions who have to figure out within an organisational context how to best work together. Teams are often jokingly described as a bit like a family; you don't really get to choose the people that you end up spending a lot of time with, except you can generally leave a workplace more easily than leaving your family! It has been suggested that it isn't so much the people we see that cause us stress, but our colleagues. Supervision time is often taken up with workers venting interpersonal frustrations or difficulties related to another staff member, colleague, manager, leader or another worker in a particular team that they are part of or connected to.

I see teams that operate well as offering good levels of communication, cohesion, cooperation, goal setting, enquiry, honesty, fun, and a commitment to working through differences. They connect and share knowledge, work collaboratively, and have clear goals and direction which together lead to a sense of team purpose and role clarity. Workers have a sense of autonomy within the team and difference in professional approaches is valued and utilised. Effective teams generally feel they have good access to resources and support, and have a sense of trust in each other's work. Humour and fun are also present so even if the nature of the work is inherently stressful at times, people enjoy going to work due to the positive interactions they have with other colleagues. As said, we spend a lot of our lives at work, if we don't like who we work with and see every day we are more likely to have significantly less enjoyment in our work. Anne Opie suggests that an effective team is 'one that attends to and works with the different knowledge of clients and their situations that are made available through discipline-specific accounts and accounts of clients and families (which may differ from each other)' (Opie 2000, p.6). She refers to teamwork as 'knowledge work' to best capture this key function of teams.

An essential part of positive and constructive teams is people being clear about their own and others' roles and clear about the work and roles of others, so these complement rather than conflict with each other. It is often a cause of frustration and resentment if people do not understand someone's role, and is usually experienced as perceiving someone is trying to take over their role or encroach on it in someway. Humans, while needing a sense of belonging, also need a sense of physical and professional ownership – something that they can claim as theirs. Just as 'hot-desking' (one desk shared among a number of staff instead of each person having their own desk) has had mixed feedback (people generally prefer even a small space they can claim as their own and return to during the day), role sharing causes difficulty for professional identity and reduces a sense of a role you can own and excel at.

Clear understanding of individual roles that acknowledges, respects, and values another person's expertise and professional knowledge is extremely important especially in multidisciplinary teams. I had a recent example in my leadership role of this, where a nurse based practitioner and a social worker almost reached a stand off due to the social worker perceiving that not only was the nurse doing the social work role at times (and not doing it in the way she would have) but there was also poor or dismissive communication around this crossing of professional role boundaries. This situation reached a point where these two professionals literally stopped talking to each other, creating a difficult tension for others on the ward to work in. People can be understandably protective over their years of training and right to do 'their job', and communication to enable role clarity is the best way to prevent this from becoming entrenched and defensive.

Another way of supporting role clarity in teams is recognising the different knowledge bases each member of the team brings. The overall aim of a team based in social service work is to develop a workable plan for a person, and if the team is multidisciplinary in nature then the aim is to bring the different discipline specific knowledge together to create a well informed plan that adjusts and flexes with the changing needs of the person it is for. This requires team members to observe value judgements or perceptions that are unhelpful about another team member's profession. Unnamed, we can see the behaviour I described above, where an undermining of the social worker's role occurred that may have been influenced by a lack of understanding or possibly a judgement or perception that their role or knowledge base wasn't as important and could be done by anyone.

This is more obvious in some organisational settings than others, such as a hospital where an unspoken hierarchy of power often exists. However, this issue must be addressed as it can result in the professionally dangerous dynamic of 'exaggerated hierarchy' (Reder, Duncan and Grey 1993) whereby a professional health worker feels they cannot challenge or disagree with another professional with more perceived power, and that somehow their knowledge is 'less than' and subsequently not contributed. Teams need to stay aware of times when one voice may be quieter than others (perhaps when someone is feeling their role is marginalised in the team) or where a dominant and fixed view is formed (often consistently by one profession) that isn't challenged. This situation can lead to frustration and dissatisfaction for individual workers. Anne Opie writes 'all disciplines, explicitly or implicitly, claim privileged knowledge, yet in all cases that knowledge is partial and can never provide the full account to which it aspires' (Opie 2000, p.8).

As team members work together and learn more about what the other does there can be a natural blurring of roles at times, usually in relation to simple tasks that can be done without a great deal of professional expertise. Key to maintaining professional safety around this is knowing your professional limits and utilising supervision to ensure you are staying within them. I find workers who run into difficulty with role clarity and boundaries are usually driven by some of the personal characteristics described at the beginning of this chapter, and their need to be 'doing' takes them too far over professional boundary lines. A simple way to bring them back is to ask them to articulate their role in one or two sentences, then to do the same with what they see is their purpose in being in the individuals or family's life, and from here let them identify where they may be going too far into another professional role.

Teams that work well respect and value the contributions of all members, and work to utilise and bring these different places of knowledge together to provide the best service possible. They also regularly look at how they are practising and at any dominant professional discourses that may have come in which are not serving them well. Team members should also not be afraid to respectfully challenge each other, using both the notion of honest honesty and appreciative enquiry techniques so a status quo that doesn't inspire innovation isn't inadvertently maintained in order to 'keep the peace'. We have individual performance appraisals but perhaps we also should have team performance appraisals. Supervision is a useful place to help workers rehearse and develop strategies to help assist with exploring possible issues and dynamics in teams, along with making personal changes that enable positive transformative change.

Another influence and impact that can occur for workers especially when they are required to be members of multi or interdisciplinary teams, is the different professional cultures they encounter. Each professional group tends to have its own 'culture', a reality we see clearly in allied health groups. It is important to try and understand professional cultures that are different to our own, and the possible influences these cultures may have on how someone else does their work. This helps us to avoid a place of judgement or reactivity to a way of working that is different to our own. Organisations that provide both interdisciplinary and individual professional development ensure excellent opportunities for greater understandings of possible professional cultures. They also allow the specific development of a professional group to enhance professional knowledge that can contribute to the service and care of people.

A regular practical impact on teams and hence workers, is as the result of staff changes, meaning the team has to move through adjusting to new members and possibly even forming, storming, norming, and performing processes identified by Bruce Tuckman in 1965, if a number of staff leave at once. This occurs in settings such as hospitals where there are rotational positions, often bringing shorter periods of team stability. Every person influences a team culture by bringing themselves to this, which is why a significant factor in recruitment processes is the consideration around 'team fit'. Employing people who will fit with the current team culture and views is often less disruptive when frequent change is occurring, and helps align the new person's own values and characteristics in the best possible way so they can work at their optimum. This also must relate to the wider context of which the team is a part, the organisational culture.

The organisation

Teams do not often exist without an organisation and the organisation doesn't exist without teams and the workers who are a part of these teams. Hence teams and the workers they are made of, exist within an organisational or agency context that may be described using such narratives as functioning, dysfunctioning, complex, enterprising, struggling, unstable supportive, innovative, marginalising, or marginalised, depending on its position and role within the wider social and political context. Workers cannot help but be impacted and influenced by how 'well' an organisation is, yet need to remember that they are in fact an integral part of the organisation and hence have significant power to influence the culture of it. All organisations have their own cultures, and it is interesting to try and describe and name this as it can often be quite historic in nature. If a worker doesn't feel they 'fit' with the culture of an organisation, this can lead to a constant sense of incongruence and displacement. In my experience, organisations that are both worker and service responsive are probably ones that fare better in recruitment, retention, and overall worker morale and satisfaction. It needs to be acknowledged that many organisations are required to show demonstrable results, but I believe the pathway to these can still be through having a focus on service and worker responsiveness.

Ways that organisations can be worker and service responsive include working from a premise of ongoing knowledge development and putting in place processes that enable continuous learning to occur. This includes making sure procedures, policies and required practices are worker and service responsive and are built with the knowledge of those who are destined to use them. Unfortunately too many procedures are often designed to manage risk adversity, leaving workers feeling they have little time to do their 'real work' as they are constantly required to be completing paperwork that keeps them trapped at their desk.

The risk of 'telling' people in infinite detail about how to do their work is that they will lose the skills and practice knowledge they have by constantly completing compliance based requirements that tell them how to do their job and allow little space for independent thinking. Organisations can forget that tools and frameworks should support the knowledge of their organisation, not drive it. The concern from this is when we really need a worker to think through a complex situation, they may have lost the ability to do so. Human service work is not predictable, tools can guide but ultimately we need to make decisions and judgements based on the uniqueness of the situation in front of us. Nigel Parton reminds us to not confuse 'tools with skills' and to 'allow ourselves space within which, no matter the speed of interactions, we can develop an understanding of others and ourselves that links us as people trying to make sense of our encounters together' (Parton 2008). The 'over proceduring' of work has consequences for creativity and stifles the potential for innovation and transformative development.

Another way to ensure worker responsiveness is to enable workers to have a sense of autonomy in what they do. While being given direction, especially when you are new to a role, is helpful, most people value organisational messages of autonomy as it is here that they feel trusted and valued in what they do. While all organisations need to have accountability systems in place (to be service responsive) these must contain a degree of logic and make sense to workers. An over compliance driven organisation does not send a message of autonomy or trust, and tends to come from an over response to something that has gone wrong. The fact that actually most of the time things go right, gets forgotten as procedures are hastily developed to prevent an infrequent mistake happening again. While we must be responsible and always learn from mistakes that occur, we shouldn't forget what is working well and further develop this. It is very hard for workers who mostly do their work well to be saddled with compliance based procedures reacting from risk averse thinking that just take up their time.

Communicating a strong organisational message about the valuing of professional development sends a powerful message about being worker responsive. Anne Opie (2000) talks about how it is an often overlooked fact that teams are located within organisations and addressing this highlights the intersection between the production of effective teamwork and organisational responsibilities for resourcing teams and ensuring members' access to professional education and ongoing training (Opie 2000, p.18).

Opportunities for professional development need to be seen as integral to an organisation, not just an inconvenient add on that takes people away from their work. I would much rather receive services from an organisation that I knew had a commitment to ongoing professional development of staff, than one that saw it as something of a time waster. Workers need time to reflect and learn and expand their knowledge and need to be part of an organisational culture that values this and sees it as essential by releasing time for people to engage in effective and management supported professional development opportunities.

This includes the need for a thorough carefully paced orientation, not just being thrown in the deep end with a cheery good luck wave and some hopeful finger crossing that you will be able to swim. The reality of a new role, new organisation, sometimes a new country, and new teams, is not something that we can easily process all at once and then go ahead and do competent work. The role of supervision and mentoring is key to a worker's orientation, and these roles are best provided by two or more different people. Mentoring helps teach and show, supervision helps reflect and deepen learning about what has been taught and provide time to process what else might be occurring. Organisations need to make these sources of professional development an absolute given, affirmed by policy, and fully mandated.

Organisations also need to have a clear set of goals and a vision about who they are there to provide a service to and where they are going. We have looked at the need for workers and teams to have role clarity and purpose, and organisations are no different. Workers need to be able to fit their professional values and direction to the culture where they work. If the organisation is unclear about this, then what can arise are pockets of different workers trying to achieve different things, and an overall lack of cohesion within the organisation. Leadership needs to take a key role here by ensuring it connects to the bigger picture of the organisational context and communicates this to all workers in ways that make sense in their work. Regular communication, down to earth language, honesty, and an active profile with staff help with this.

Workers often bring issues of leadership to supervision as, due to the organisational authority given to it, leadership can have direct impact on a worker and hence is also a very scrutinised role. It is difficult to work in a team where you don't agree with the leadership or you see it as harmful or negative, such as bullying, passive, and not focused on the team of people it is serving. I will talk more about the role of leadership in relation to supervision in Chapter 8, and at this point suggest that leaders must be available, approachable and visibly seen as actively worker and service responsive.

If leaders are not seen as especially responsive or lacking in emotional and social awareness workers are more likely to reduce their expectations of this person and discontinue seeking their advice unless they absolutely have to. If they show a lack of sensitivity to workers through high demand with little or no acknowledgment, and a constant focus on outputs (especially if this also mirrors the message of the organisation) workers tend to withdraw and eventually leave. Organisations need to be people centred with a clear direction and focus – not too narrow (confining) and not too broad (confusing).

A key way for organisations to remain service focused is to engage consumer views or the opinions of those they are providing a service to. Just as workers tend to get annoyed and frustrated when handed a decision that directly impacts on their work that no one asked their input on, so too do those who we serve. Organisations who are informed by those who use their services are more likely to be service responsive. This may also include organisations and the need for multi agency collaboration. There is at times a nervousness that working closely with another organisation will mean a loss of identity, especially if the organisation is significantly bigger. However, diversity is one of the best factors organisations can provide. No one we work with is the same, so having a range of services to connect people with is enriching and helpful to best meet their needs. Expecting everyone to work the same way as us is not especially useful, it is preferable we find ways to best work with other organisations, not expect them to conform to our expectations.

Organisations have to work within financial constraints and this is especially evident in social service type work, namely health and welfare. In Anne Opie's study of effective teams most participants commented that a lack of resourcing affected the teams' effectiveness because there were insufficient resources in the community to which they could refer clients (Opie 2000, p.114). Many social service agencies tend to operate from a sense of scarcity which may turn into a fight to procure resources especially if they are expected to operate within an outcome focused context and must literally prove their worth through business model type thinking or reporting. This can lead to some protectiveness about agencies 'gate keeping' and not sharing resources in a bid to make them last longer. Workers may complain about another organisations not sharing resources (information, time, etc.) and not doing what they perceive their job to be.

Jan Horwath and Tony Morrison explore interagency working in their article on collaboration, integration and change in children's services (2007), suggesting a history of positive informal networking can be a positive influence when agencies are required to work more closely together, along with shared values, building trust, role clarity, role security and respect, communication, shared training, and having clear qualitative, measured over time outcomes

(Horwath and Morrison 2007, p.6). As supervisors, we can help workers build and develop these factors which interestingly mirror what is required to work effectively in teams.

Organisations also need to take care with the amount of restructuring and change they put workers through in response to usually external influences. Workers can easily get change fatigued which presents through cynicism, and resistance to change. Sometimes it can feel that each new chief executive officer or chief operations officer arrives and feels the need to stamp their mark on the organisation. Views of staff are sought belatedly or not sought at all, and the change arrives as potential criticism of the way work is currently being done without clear signals that the way work is currently done is understood. Organisations also seem to make superficial annoying changes while a conservative core essentially remains the same. If staff cannot see the logic behind a change they are less likely to engage with it especially if it carries a threat to job security. While we accept that change is a fact of life, it helps if it is seen to have meaning, purpose, focus and direction, and with worker input. It needs to carry forward what is working well, not just toss everything out. As supervisors we need to be alert to change fatigue in workers and the risk this carries of contributing to feelings of burnout and staff leaving.

The final two influences I want to discuss that impact or influence workers are media scrutiny and the actual physical working environment. I will discuss our current global context and the impacts of this in the next chapter. Organisations operate in a political climate that will be influenced by the focus of the government in power and the wider economic climate. Organisations may come under scrutiny depending on what pressures or initiatives the government is choosing to address. This type of scrutiny can lead to funding changes and new performance measures, and especially public government funded organisations retreating from innovation to risk adverse type thinking and management. A key player in this is the media. Not only is social service work emotive for those requiring its services and those providing these, but when something happens (generally negative) the media can highlight and trigger an emotive response from the wider public which will inevitably fall back on the government of the time. The fear of suddenly being put on public display if you make a mistake becomes heightened if you work in an organisation that the media has turned its eye to. I would suggest that possibly one of the most stressful events that can occur for a worker is to be part of an event that leads to serious injury or death. This alone is deeply crippling, but the media focus that follows can effectively seal the fate of a person's career.

There is no denying that our work is often carried out on a public stage. We all have the responsibility to work safely and remain accountable to those that we provide a service to. Organisations can best support workers to do this through staying aware of the expectations and working conditions they provide, such as sufficient leave provision (and opportunities to take it), having constructive and supportive professional development and workforce development structures in place and always learning from mistakes and successes. At the micro level, this is what supervision is about, and as painful as mistakes can be, they do provide some of our most powerful learning.

My final comment on workplace influences and impacts is directed at the physical working environment that is provided. In our overcrowded world I am becoming more and more aware of the concrete neon lit structures we ask people to work in. Windowless rooms with no natural light, constant noise, shared desks, shabby peeling walls, smells, cramped office space and frustrating technology all impact on workers. We forget sometimes that we are physical beings, sensitive to the physical energies that emanate from certain environments. Often through lack of resources we settle for poor working conditions that cause workers to escape (eventually unproductively) at the first opportunity. Rules such as depersonalised clear desks leave work environments devoid of what personally matters to us and create no sense of belonging. We are physical, emotional, and spiritual beings and our physical environment will impact negatively or positively on these facets of ourselves. As Abraham Maslow showed us in his hierarchy of needs, we cannot attend to our higher process of self actualisation if our basic physical needs are not well met. Organisations do need to think carefully about the physical environments they provide for workers.

Working with resilience

Resiliency theory offers us a helpful way to explore, support and strengthen the interaction between a worker and their work environment, and help manage the influences and impacts of this. Resilience involves both personal intra and inter personal protective process that help manage environmental influences and impacts. Rather than resiliency being seen as something you have or don't have, supervisors can stay alert to what it looks like in the workplace, and help enhance strengths that a worker brings to enable and enhance resiliency. Froma Walsh talks about it being a common misconception that resiliency means invulnerability. Neither is resilience the ability to 'bounce back unscathed', rather, she suggests it is 'struggling well, effectively working through and learning from adversity, and integrating the experience into the fabric of individual and shared life passage' (Walsh 2008, p.6).

As supervisors it is important that we are able to recognise what workers already do that supports resiliency for them in the context of their work environment and identify areas where we could help them develop their resilient responses. This includes recognising and supporting the emotional expression of what may have occurred and assisting this to not become a permanent set back or negative state. Al Siebert refers to resilience in the workplace as the ability to 'cope with ongoing disruptive change, sustain good physical and emotional health when under constant pressure, bounce back easily from setbacks, overcome adversities, change to a new way of working and living when an old way is no longer working, and do all this without acting in a dysfunctional or harmful way' (Siebert 2006, p.4).

He also talks about the importance of workplaces providing workers with a sense that their work is important and meaningful, that they have responsibilities, are recognised for achievements, receive opportunities for personal growth, are valued and appreciated and are accomplishing something (2006, p.4). As supervisors we can certainly highlight and reinforce these areas so workers are better sustained in the work they undertake. This can also help lead to a change in perspective or perception that may be hindering or holding a person back. As workers in organisations, there are some things we can't easily change, but it is hoped that we can change how we respond to them.

Another key area that supports resiliency in managing workplace adversity is evidence through trauma recovery that shows the importance of talking over, sharing stories, connecting with others, receiving reassurance and comfort and experiencing empathy and safety with others to help with this. Froma Walsh discusses how these sorts of processes help to counter feelings of insecurity, helplessness, and meaninglessness (Walsh 2008, p.8). It is interesting reflecting on this here in New Zealand in the wake of two large and devastating earthquakes in our second biggest city, Christchurch. Certainly these feelings are some of what people who are unable to process these traumatic events have experienced. Froma Walsh lists key practice principles to help strengthen family resilience some of which I have adapted to be able to be used by supervisors to support workplace resilience especially when adversity has been encountered:

- Express that you believe in the supervisee's ability to overcome adversity.
- Be compassionate and provide a safe place to talk.
- Listen and don't judge the person.
- Ask questions using the emotional awareness and intuitive processes.
- Humanise and contextualise distress using normalising, decreasing stigma and blame.
- Identify and build strengths alongside vulnerabilities.
- Identify other resources they can utilise for support.

- Shift focus from problems to possibilities – be creative and support adaptation.

- Identify next action steps to help someone begin to move forward.

- Ask them to name the personal practice theory they are taking away from the experience.

(Adapted from Walsh 2008, p.12)

Using this type of approach we can again see the importance of the supervisory relationship to create a 'safe place' whereby a worker can seek this type of support and hence provide a preventative and protective space against some of these lasting effects. This also needs to be reinforced by other organisational supports such as peer support, debriefing, leadership support and time to process the event. As mentioned in Chapter 2, humour also supports resiliency, and organisations that provide opportunities for fun, relaxation, and social connection can help mitigate some of the impacts of difficult work on their workers. When we feel out of control or over controlled for whatever reason we tend to either look for structure or places we can have a say, some control, or choice. As supervisors we can help workers identify where these places might be or help them bring more of a sense of structure such as identifying the places where they can still have control even if this is in some small way.

Conclusion

Supervisors need to remain aware of the work environment that supervisees work within, and support workers to identify ways of responding to the impacts and influences around them. This can help us build greater understanding of the worker and help us take care in working from where a worker may be at and what change is realistic in their given circumstance. Supervisors can help workers debrief, explore, and make sense of the environment they are a part of. Developing emotional and intuitive awareness supports this, along with normalising or exploring solutions to conflict and difficulty. Bringing forward more of the transformative function in supervision can also mean supervision is innovative and exciting, which are all good counters to some of the possible worker environmental impacts and influences discussed. A key way of supporting this is the message supervisors can provide that even though you may not be able to change another person, you can change how you respond to them or what is happening. Alongside being aware of worker characteristics, team influences and the wider organisational context, supervisors must also remain aware of the global influences and impacts that our society is operating in. This awareness is part of gaining a greater understanding of the wider dynamics present for us all in our work.

Chapter 7

Global Influences

No army can withstand the strength of an idea whose time has come.

Victor Hugo 1802–1885

The human race is at a crossroads of change and survival that requires us all to step up to addressing how we live in the world. Echart Tolle writes in his book *A New Earth* – 'Driven by greed, ignorant of their connectedness to the whole, humans persist in behaviour that, if continued unchecked, can only result in their own destruction' (2005, p.11). The loudest voice in our world is that of economic globalisation where international markets influence and impact on us all especially through the increased communication and technological advances of our world. This chapter will explore this wider global context that supervision operates in along with current global trends, and name possible impacts and influences on workers that as supervisors we need to be aware of and sensitive to.

Globalisation

While globalisation, including the ability to travel across the world within a day, and to communicate instantly with someone in another country, has reduced the notion of separateness, it has also possibly spawned a desire to even more tightly manage and protect one's own sense of space, culture, identity, and resources. If globalisation is also defined and initiated by economic forces, then what it can do is ensure the loudest economic voices have the greatest power, and they create systems and processes to ensure this. Kieran O'Donoghue (2003) writes that 'primarily the global economic voice is concerned with capitalist development and the privatisation of wealth on a global scale' and says the 'economic voice is the dominant global voice' (p.62). Unfortunately the economic motivation that is largely behind the destruction and pollution of our planet as countries seek to increase profit margins, has never had the long term survival of our planet at its heart. Instead it seeks exploitive and competitive means that only benefit a few to answer a need for wealth and power.

The impact of changing market forces is now felt by all of us. As we come through a world recession we are aware of how much we are impacted on by the decisions made by others. Even living at the bottom of the world, the impact of the recession was felt here in New Zealand. I became acutely aware that I live in a small country that is dependent on trade agreements as part of its economic survival. As economic belts tighten, all services are required to show their market worth, creating the 'business-isation' of what were service based agencies. As discussed, we see business language creep in, leading workers to struggle with maintaining the integrity of their work amid productivity demands, key performance indicators, and persistent messages about outputs.

As governments in power change, the left or right direction of these brings their own economic influences which are exerted through their time in office. Workers fight back to protect standards of living and to look after their own, our sense of economic survival becomes our main focus and at times reduces our willingness to help others, instead keeping energy for ourselves. We become located firmly in an individualised way of thinking of 'I' and 'mine', and lose sense of our global responsibility, instead becoming self oriented.

The short term reality of surviving does not provide for a longer term survival plan for our earth. For workers, particularly those providing a service to those who may have fewer resources, their work becomes traumatic when 'witnessing of social phenomena such as gender violence, hunger and poverty' (Profitt 2008, p.160). Exposure to the differences inherent in our society, lack of equity, and impact of historical colonisation, engenders either an increased awareness of social injustice, or a form of discounting based on how overwhelming and complex the issues seem and our helplessness in the face of this. It may also cause a sense of shame or guilt about having access to what others do not. This too can result in an inability to act, as workers become uncomfortably aware of their own sense of privilege. A response can be to blame and become angry at those who don't appear to help themselves. But what is really required is a place of understanding to learn how the person came to be in this place and the wider social economic dynamics that have contributed to it.

Sir Mason Durie in his keynote speech at the International Federation of Social Work (IFSW) conference in Auckland in 2009 commented that we cannot separate economic and social policies as these are bound by the 'twin pillars of want and need'. This is evident in the ongoing struggle to fight poverty in especially developing countries, emphasised by food shortages and further impacted on by global climate change. Forced into an economic global game that undoes ways of living and knowledge of surviving for hundreds of years, some of these cultures are becoming lost in a desperate bid to survive, losing not only those within them but also generational indigenous wisdom. Sir Mason Durie spoke of this as also the concept 'global colonisation' meaning through increased travel and technology we have greater access to other cultures, but this also increases the risk of losing cultural distinctiveness, an example being the loss of native languages. Inherent in global poverty is the loss of fundamental human rights such as a lack of access to education, and health care – this results in massive inequality being evident across our world. Issues of over population of our world are also forcing economic and social issues into a closer connection.

A noisy place

As a spin off from economic globalisation, there are massive technological advances occurring every day. We are all aware of how rapidly our technological world is changing. Barely do we come to terms with a new cell phone or computer program, when another one emerges that does more, is faster, has more capacity, and ultimately seeks to enable greater connectivity. What is interesting about this is the irony of how Eckhart Tolle (2005) suggests that is it through a lack of connectedness that humans continue to ignorantly destroy the planet we inhabit.

Rapid fire communication now provides quick snapshots of a person's world. We can send instant updates and texts on our cell phones, and go online to change our profiles on social networking sites, and all this keeps communication at a superficial level of human engagement. It also sets up what Kieran O'Donoghue calls a 'culture of immediacy' (2003, p.63). We expect communication and results to occur immediately, our low tolerance for times when things don't happen fast enough or our computer breaks down gives rise to an almost technological rage, not dissimilar to road rage. Our patience, tolerance and expectations are being subtly altered by the world of communication based technology that we exist in. While speeding up communication processes can be helpful, and idea exchange easier and wider reaching, something is changing in how we interact as human beings. I also think there is a subtle stress of always being available and contactable, that we are not paying enough attention to.

I call this living in a world of noise. Aside from the obvious noise of living in busy cities, we have created noise through technology that demands we be available. I don't believe human beings are designed to always have to be in interaction. We all need places of quiet to re-group in ourselves, to process, and to make sense of events and experiences. We need to learn how to be on our own so we can be at one with ourselves. To always be surrounded by some type of noise keeps this possibility at bay, and I believe impacts on our ability to manage when things perhaps don't go well. Human beings are interdependent, we begin as dependent, our journey to adulthood is about learning independence from our parents, and then we learn the power of interdependence, where we come to see our connectedness not just to each other but to the entire world. We need time to stand in a forest, at the beach, in the mountains, and inhale the air of serenity. We need to create our own special places be that through music or gardening or other peaceful heart centred activities. Our noisy crowded worlds of technology and instant communication instead create a sense of belonging based on dependency, which does not grow this skill in us. It heightens our reactivity because our restorative times are becoming smaller.

A materialistic focus

With predominantly economic forces controlling our world, it is not surprising that a key to their continuation is the power of marketing. Marketing helps us believe that accumulation of wealth or objects will somehow make us feel happier and provide a sense of belonging. We are constantly told to be dissatisfied with what we have and what is wrong with it and then sold something to address these shortcomings. Instead of messages about finding security and belonging within us, we are fed the short thrill of acquisition. When this wears off, like an addiction we feel dissatisfied and go and get something else to meet this need. Our individualised societies with their subtle or not subtle class systems tell us we are measured by our wealth, our work, and our status. This is all based on the power of comparison. So often, discontent and frustration in our lives is due to looking at something or someone and comparing ourselves to them. Comparing is possibly the greatest source of discontent that I think exists. And it is the backbone of materialist behaviour that supports our economic and market forces.

Objects don't make us happy. Our work does if it is our true work and something we get to live out our true selves within. Loving and being loved does bring happiness, but an over attachment to happiness will inevitably fail. Nothing goes right all of the time, life is hard and contains loss, we are all going to die. It is ok to have things that may make our life easier at times in someway, or that we enjoy in terms of their beauty or design, but all this can be destroyed in a flood or earthquake and we find that actually we can live without these things, because that is what people do. They are not what defines us, they are merely items that will come and go. If our self esteem is invested in objects we will always be somewhat unhappy because deep down we will be caught in a comparative game of superficial fulfilment trying to meet dissatisfaction and insecurity. We will, however, be very popular with sales people and those in marketing!

We also currently have a shocking paradigm in the world where people are dying from the effects of too little and too much food. On a global level we see this in the stark contrast between developed and developing countries with people dying of both the health consequences of obesity and malnutrition. In the Western world we have people struggling with eating healthily where food has become a massive industry. We have access to cheap processed food sold through convincing marketing that promises instant fulfilment and contentment. These types of foods also tend to be priced to be more accessible than healthier options especially for those struggling financially. The satisfaction they offer tends to be short lived and these instant foods deplete rather than meet our health needs. Once out of balance with a healthy weight, we then have billion dollar weight and beauty industries prepared to sell us diets and ways to become an ideal weight again. The simple rules of eating healthily and exercising are often lost beneath layers of products and promises of quick fixes resulting in weight cycling that remains out of balance. For some people food can also become a defence, and a way to assert control, or alternatively, provides a short term 'filling up' or comfort to address anxiety, loneliness, unhappiness and low self esteem. It can indicate a possible disconnection between body and mind when this spirals into a form of addiction and disorder.

Violence and fear

Along with the impacts of poverty and lack of equity in our societies and world, is the harsh presence of violence. Violence is a display of power by those whose power feels threatened. When stripped back, it represents a fear of something being taken or a loss of control. From a child who hits another because he felt powerless and couldn't think of another way to end a situation, to a country that retaliates to a threat or attack, the dynamic is the same. Something is threatened, someone feels powerless, and someone acts to show their power, then violence occurs. This may appear basic and possibly too simplistic a representation of the social complexities that also exist, but I fundamentally believe that violence is a response to one of our most innate emotions, our fear.

Violence can occur on an individual, family, societal, and global level. It can be evident in acts of partner and child abuse, gangs, inter racial conflicts, and wars. Whatever the way it is displayed, violence in my experience is always about fear and a sense of powerlessness. It is a means to get back a sense of control and power that is perceived to have been taken or reduced, or is perceived to be at threat. It can be seen through the use of religion to justify violence, where an over identification to a religious way of being leads some to extreme measures to defend a fear of this been challenged or overthrown. A conviction of being absolutely right may come from a fear of other beliefs that may challenge or dispute this, and a lack of willingness to consider an alternative view. Somewhere in there is a fear of something being taken or lost to cause such extreme acts to defend it.

If we were able to recognise the fear that sits behind so much of our reactive behaviour, we would reduce the power of it. Fear has a natural purpose to keep us safe and alert to danger, but when used to reassert some form of perceived loss of power, it only causes devastation. When displayed at children it sends a message of how to get what you want in the world and that being violent and exerting more control is the only way to achieve this. Violence directed at children sets up a biological way of responding to the world that is located in fear. We have children who grow up with heightened cortisol and adrenalin responses who are frequently physically reacting in an unregulated way to situations because their nervous systems are too highly cued to danger.

Our prisons are full of people who are actually disabled in their emotional regulation due to being too highly biologically programmed to danger resulting in short term survival based thinking and reactivity. This is predominantly a result of early trauma usually connected to violence. Until we treat the source of powerlessness that occurs for people who seek violence as a way of managing the unbearable sense of feeling out of control and disempowered, we will continue to have crime and the resulting devastation to people's lives. Until we are prepared to recognise our commonalities, respect our differences, and share our resources, we will have wars.

Depression

It is not surprising that people can feel lost and confused amid the noise and demand of an ever changing world. When we look about it all seems so overwhelming with so many messages about how to live our lives. We naturally choose to invest our energies in one place be this work and or family as a way of having a sense of purpose and focus. This is fine as long as we don't become over defined by these roles and lose our true voice to an expectation of them. Otherwise one day we can wake up and find we are retired or the children have all gone out into the world, and we panic because we have no sense of who we now are. A deep centred fear of possibly not being worthwhile is triggered. We try and cling tightly to old ways of being and thinking that may no longer serve us well. A consequence of this can be depression, and along with the health impacts of poor nutrition, lack of exercise, and violence, the Western world faces a steady increase in the presentation of this mental illness.

Having lived through a severe episode of major clinical depression that lasted for a year when I was 30, I am well aware of the impact of depression and how debilitating it is. I offer my view on it framed from my experience and it is important to note this will be different for other people. I see depression as first an emotional and psychological condition that then has biological involvement causing an alteration to serotonin levels in the brain. Genetic components may also mean some people are possibly more likely to experience depression.

My depression was a combination of a genetic predisposition, a highly wired central nervous system contributing to anxiety and sensitivity, of living with very high standards and expectations (my own), and of never having worked constructively with anger. My depression was quite sudden in onset yet had a clearly marked pathway leading up to it. The key loss for me was of my hope. I woke up after a bizarre night experience where I thought I was dying and falling, to having absolutely no hope and everything feeling like it had lost colour. I felt like I had fallen into a very dark abyss and I couldn't see a way to climb out of it.

When I did the work to get through depression with the help of a wonderful psychotherapist, Mary Wilson, I saw the journey that had contributed to it including always living too fast and too far ahead. I was never really present or relaxed. I also saw the conditioning that told me to repress anger and instead to be sad or fearful. With being so caught in achieving as a means of defining myself and going so far ahead in my thoughts and actions, it was almost like my body and brain one day said 'We've had enough, you have to stop and look, and get more present, and these old ways of doing things are no longer serving you well.'

It was like walking into a very high brick wall that didn't yield and from which I had to painfully pull all the bricks out in order to get through. Through a loss of appetite and inability to sleep, I lost a serious amount of weight and in a way this symbolised a shedding of my no longer helpful personal constructs, the drama, the action, the roles and performance that I had been caught in. Depression slows you down (actually it makes you so slow you just about stop!) and it makes you look. When we truly take the courage to look at what we are afraid of and what we have constructed to manage this, we learn what isn't serving us well.

There was a wonderful moment I will never forget when I realised I was coming through my depression. I was at a beach here in New Zealand with a friend and the sun was just starting to go down. We were walking along the shoreline and we saw a young fur seal in the shallow waters seemingly having difficulty getting out beyond the surf. We ran over and were joined by another couple of people who said that he had been around the beach for the last couple of days and not to worry, a local ranger had told them that he was the age and stage of being able to be out on his own. We all stood there and watched him fighting the waves and being tossed backwards and forwards, and then, just like that, suddenly he made it and was swimming away. We all broke into spontaneous applause and I realised I was smiling. I felt peaceful, connected, and utterly present. I felt hopeful.

Depression is often about suppression and repression; of ourselves, our voice, our emotions, our fears, and our experiences. For me it was also about anger turned inward and I had never realised how empowering it is to get angry (directed out safely of course). Our world has many controls and we also control ourselves, sometimes too much, and at the risk of our mental wellbeing. We suppress ourselves in fear of rejection or overwhelm and throw ourselves into roles that can also deny us. When we are in our true 'work' it doesn't feel as if we are working because it is like living out our true purpose. It feels right, and maybe occasionally hard or challenging, but ok. This is because we are being congruent and present and open. We are truly there and available and others recognise this about us. We still follow social norms and rules but these do not rule us. Depression is a sign that we are out of balance and we need to look. It cannot be covered up with food, objects, status, roles or using other people to meet our needs. The increase of depression in our world tells me that people are feeling internally and spiritually out of balance and that the way we are treating the world is also out of balance.

A supervision context of hope

While some of these global impacts and influences can feel overwhelming, we must always hold hope and send messages of this within the supervision context. Yes we live in a challenging world environment that seems to conspire against the bringing forward of our true selves, and we see and hear things happening in the world that are distressing and upsetting. Amid this workers need to remain positive about the change they can bring to the world and emotionally listen for when they are feeling overwhelmed and when this is affecting their work. 'What do you need to retain perspective, hope, and an understanding of the social inequalities that underpin so much violence and distress?' is a great suggested question asked by Allyson Davys and Liz Beddoe (2010, p.231) that supervisors can utilise. I would add, what do you like about your work, what brings you hope, what are the places in your work where you feel you make a change, and what is it in your work that connects with who you are?

As supervisors we need to be able to congruently message our hope. This requires us to be always reflecting and using our own supervision to be exploring how we are in our roles and work. I had an experience with a supervisee who was expressing frustration and cynicism at the mismatch she saw about what we promise in health and what we deliver. This appeared to stem from a place of helplessness relating to someone she knew experiencing a rapid decline in their health and dying. The worry was that her staying in this place would lead her to be cynical and less convinced of the value of her own work.

That week I had just done a notes audit for another social worker and was browsing through the medical file looking out for the social worker's entries (that were actually in the prior admission notes) when suddenly the clinical notes ended with 'May her soul rest in peace'. This gave me quite a shock, as while I had been realising the woman was dying I didn't expect death to have come so soon. I back tracked and read the last couple of entries which showed a level of care and attentiveness to both this woman and her family that made tears come to my eyes. It reminded me of the dedication of hospital personnel and the human qualities of compassion and caring that are so often present in health work. I felt very heartened reading this.

I decided to share this experience with my supervisee and told her about my emotional response to it. I said it reminded me that sometimes there is nothing we can do, but that hospital staff still do a valuable and powerful job at those times especially when they really bring themselves into their work. My sharing this with her seemed to create a shift as it helped her soften some of the defensive response she had developed in terms of her own helplessness, and we went on to talk further about this and about being courageous when faced with an outcome no one would have hoped for. I have already talked in Chapter 2 about how as supervisors we can use professional and personal disclosure and this also relates to our hope and moments that confirm this for us. We need to have confidence, belief and hope in our work and in the worker. This will help them also have hope when they are experiencing some of the difficult contextual experiences discussed.

There is a strengths based practice principle that says we must believe all people are capable of growth and change. This sounds simple but I have found it is not applied to everyone. Sometimes our personal and social constructs lead us to be selective about who may change and who might not. For example, we might think someone could change their tendency to shoplift but not another person who sexually offends against children. There are some behaviours or conditions that can cause workers to have less hope in change or none at all. I have mentioned obesity, and this may be another area where workers could become cynical or doubting, also influenced by cultural or socioeconomic projections and assumptions.

As supervisors we need to help workers examine their beliefs and values around where change is and is not possible, as this is often about hope. If we don't really believe a person can change their behaviour, this will become evident in our motivation to work with them. A worker may have mentally given up and tossed away the possibility of making change and a person will sense and pick up on this. If it is not possible for a worker to have this type of hope and belief in change then it may be best someone else works with the person. It is the same with global, organisational, and team impacts and influences.

We need to help the worker examine what sits behind a possible lack of hope and then assist them to identify places where even small change could be achieved. Helplessness and loss of hope often arise from feeling overwhelmed and not being able to see anything that can be done. Even writing a letter to a politician is one positive step that can help free up this feeling of powerlessness and help a worker regain a sense of being proactive in their work. The many means of communication available to us are such that we can rally support around an idea or raise a voice that needs to be heard.

Conclusion

Although there are undoubtedly huge challenges in our world today there are many good things happening to address these. John Langmore suggests that in relation to globalisation there is 'much evidence of socially and economically responsible and innovative thinking, and that this is a time of opportunity'. He comments that we can all 'help shape the future through imaginative re thinking and firm, authoritative social action, service, and advocacy... we can all be influential on movement towards a more humane, just, peaceful and inclusive global society' (cited in Jackson and Segal 2002, p.25). Workers need to be both socially and economically aware, realising as Sir Mason Durie states, that we must consider these in connection to each other especially in the area of policy development.

Realisation of our impact on the planet is causing people to be more responsible, to consider less harmful ways of being in the world, to think about the environment with new eyes and to take better care of it. It is teaching us to be responsible beyond our immediate circle of family and friends, and that we must work together to stop and help repair the damage we have done to the planet. We are seeing more collective responses to issues that help counter a competitive short term thinking, gain driven focus. These are becoming more evident locally, regionally, nationally and globally. There is a new consciousness that is arising that recognises the importance of connectedness and this is helping lower the barriers of difference that are often created.

We are speaking out against violence and realise the enormous harm it creates not only now but in generations to come. This includes challenging and sending alternative messages so children and people are not harmed through people's use of violence. People are realising, sometimes through the impact of natural disasters, what really matters, and the power of community, locally, nationally, and internationally. We are addressing the stigmatisation of mental illness and opening doors to wider social support and responsiveness to this.

As Mahatma Gandhi said we must 'be the change we want to see in the world' (Exley 1999, p.88). As supervisors we need to stay aware of the contexts that both we and workers are operating in. We must bring analysis to our work that can recognise the impact and influences of these from the level of worker characteristics, to the organisational context, the societies we are a part of, and the world that we must all work together to protect. For transformative work to occur we must be prepared to bring the very best of us to help workers bring the very best of them, and be prepared to not only talk but walk the pathway of transformative change. This requires supervisors to be leaders; a function that I believe is inherent in the supervisor role, which will be explored further in the next chapter.

Chapter 8

Supervisors as Leaders

Man is not on the earth solely for his own happiness.
He is there to realise great things for humanity.
Vincent van Gogh 1853–1890

An area of supervision that is not always addressed is the leadership role. Because it should ideally be separate from line management (and if supervisors are in leadership roles, this is acknowledged and managed), supervision is not often seen in the formal leadership realm. Yet in my opinion supervisors are an organisation's practice leaders as they are helping steer the direction of practice, and influence the culture of support and professional development on a one to one level. To be a supervisor generally requires at least three years in practice which again means a supervisor is already more advanced in their experience.

The organisation has given authority to supervisors to provide supervision as a key component of professional development and support, thus giving supervisors the power to perform this function. To do this well and engage in transformative work that will support wider positive change, I believe it is time for supervisors, often as quiet leaders, to step forward and up to the challenges of leadership. This chapter will explore ways to do this, beginning with discussing the concept of transformative leadership, exploring the roles of teaching, leading, and supervising, the concept of adaptive leadership, and leadership styles and traits. It will conclude with considering ways for supervisors to be actively involved in personal and professional development including a simple self reflection tool.

Transformative leadership

Leadership should be about aiming beyond ourselves and always for the betterment of others. Joseph Jaworski describes transformational leadership as having strong commitments and broad visionary ideas, the idea of service and compassion for others, the idea of helping others in their struggle to break free of their limits (1996, p.59). He talks about leadership being about the release of human possibilities and conveying this belief in your communication – to move people, pull them into the activity, help get them centred and focused at operating at peak capacity (1996, p.66). This sounds remarkably like what should occur in supervision, where the focus is on the supervisee and the supervisor helps motivate, inspire and identify ways to improve and enhance work and helps a pathway of action to become clear.

The importance of focus cannot be understated. When we are truly focused on another we are present, we are engaging in the U theory of sensing, opening, letting go and letting come. How I describe this in the supervision I provide is about being attentive. I literally make myself focus on the person by noticing their energy, behaviour, and I look into their eyes. I can feel my whole self attending to them and bringing both them and me into the room. The power of attention is enormous, it makes people feel validated, their experiences substantiated, their importance recognised. It is like saying 'I see you' with every form of communication you have. This of course is best done with humour and warmth so it isn't so intense the person wants to run screaming from the room! It isn't about trying so hard it becomes forced, it is an alertness, a recognising, it is about being respectfully present for another person.

Leaders help change how people think about things, they increase options, take risks, and are bold. Abraham Zaleznik in his 1977 article on managers and leaders describes leaders as artists: tolerating chaos and lack of structure, and having the ability to influence the thoughts and actions of other people (Zaleznik 1977, p.2). He talks about leaders being referred to with adjectives rich in emotional content saying 'leaders attract strong feelings of identity and difference or of love and hate' (p.8) and that they change how people think about what's desirable and possible, relating to people 'directly, intuitively and empathetically' (p.1).What he makes clear throughout his article is the difference between managers and leaders. Managers need to manage the day to day operational functioning of an organisation, their role is important and essential to ensure things get done and run smoothly. Leaders need managers to move ideas into action and make them happen on a day to day basis. In this chapter I am describing supervisors as practice leaders, not practice managers as I believe it is here that the confusion of supervision being another form of line management arises. I am suggesting supervisors be practice leaders who work with ideas, insight, foresight, take risks and open up opportunities in another's personal and professional development.

My thinking about supervisors as leaders was reinforced by reading the aims of the American Leadership Forum which Joseph Jaworski was central to developing. I have adapted these aims to be applicable to what we as supervisors can strive for in our roles as practice leaders. Here is the adapted list:

1. Help strengthen self belief and self efficacy in those that we supervise.

2. Encourage supervisees to rely on their inner resources, to use their intuition and harness the ability to be innovative especially in times of change or difficulty.

3. Help supervisees to be proactive in teamwork, to support collaboration and connection within and beyond their organisation.

4. Challenge supervisees to reach deeply into themselves and connect with the wider human consciousness that supports them in the work they do with others and to promote personal and professional development.

5. Support supervisees to learn from their practice experience about how to be flexible, resilient, and adapt quickly to change and new environments.

(Adapted from 'Aims of the American Leadership Forum', Jaworski 1996, p.101)

This list could easily become a set of principles and aims of transformative supervision, and is exciting in how meeting these aims would in turn grow leadership qualities in those that we supervise. Leadership is always about taking others with you, never being the sole place of reliance for people. It is strengthening workers to essentially lead themselves. We should never build dependence; everything we do must be done so others can do it when we are not there.

Teacher, leader, supervisor

The second aim of the American Leadership Forum as seen above captures the idea that supervisors are not required to be experts in everything, but instead to help workers discover their own solutions to issues. This is described by Norcross and Halgin 1997 as being about 'how to think' rather than 'what to think' (Falender and Shafranske 2004, p.232). In some ways the word ' leader' suggests a 'leading to' and we need to take care we are leading people to explore and build their own knowledge based on a process of self awareness and discovery, not just leading them to ours. This is the idea of teaching, which isn't about just providing answers; it is about helping people find their own answers through how we ask questions. A supervisor may, as teachers do, offer some ideas into the learning process, but always from a place of offering rather than telling. We are always more likely to own knowledge that we have helped discover through our own process of application and the testing out of ideas and information.

This reflects a key part of engaging in transformative work, which is the application and bringing to life, the new realisation, insight, and awareness. This might be as subtle as a change in reaction or thought, or as obvious as a deliberately tried new technique or skill. As supervisors we need to ask and celebrate the application of the insight that has come into action. I always think it is brave when a worker goes and tries a new way of thinking, behaving, and working and notices the further shift that comes. Often this presents back as excitement and we don't even have to ask as the supervisee can't wait to tell us their discovery! This is the place of developing and expanding personal practice theory and we should never lose the opportunity to congratulate someone in taking a step of change, just as we should also embrace the opportunity to raise a challenge or counter consideration if we see a gap or potential opportunity for development.

I had both of these instances occur where a supervisee came into supervision and shared how she had applied our newly introduced screening questions around partner abuse. We explored how she had done this, how she felt about it, and her confidence was high about having given it a go. I was really pleased because it isn't easy work and she had done the screening well. In listening to the description and subsequent plan I also became aware of a practice gap that had been missed which was not taking a particular and very important act around protecting the children. I could see what had potentially happened; in her determination to do the screening well she had become solely adult focused and hadn't quite factored in the children who were witnessing violence.

I had a responsibility to comment on this but I knew it was going to potentially deflate the excitement she had experienced. What I said was: 'I think it is so great how you took the courage to give the screening questions a go, and your determination on getting the mum safe, I am wondering little though, about the children?' That was all I needed to say. Her eyes widened in horror and she threw her hands up to her face and went 'Oh my God, oh no, I forgot about the children.' She was almost inconsolable and when I (in an attempt to make her feel better) started to say 'It's ok...' she said 'It's not ok Nicki!' I hastily said, 'It's ok to have made a mistake so how can we remedy it?' She immediately came up with a plan and straight after supervision put it into action.

Learning from mistakes is often used as a catch phrase, however, it does take reflection to occur first in order to explore what happened to contribute to the mistake. Once actions, thoughts, reactions are identified and named, I find they are then able to be transformed into positive new ways of responding to or doing something. Leaders do not hammer people about their mistakes but we should expect learning to occur and be prepared to model this in everything we do. I find in my leadership position that if I am prepared to put my mistakes and fallible moments (of which there are many!) out there, this actually helps people come forward around their own.

Leaders sometimes worry that they always have to be perfect or a shining example. We are becoming shining examples by honestly sharing when we don't get it right. A culture of openness is a far better place to bring about positive change, than a suppressing place around the fear of been judged. Dr Andrew Turnell (Turnell and Edwards 1999) said 'We have to make judgments about behaviour and safety, but the final judgment of someone isn't ours.' This is true, while we have the responsibility to pick up on practice that perhaps needs to be stronger and safer in some way, it is not up to me to judge anyone, that is way beyond my human brief. In my life sometimes the outcomes which at the time I really didn't want to be the way they were, have been, on reflection, exactly what they should have been, to help me let go and move to a different pathway.

Adaptive leadership

Ronald Heifetz and Donald Laurie talk about the importance of the adaptive function of leadership, whereby rather than just imparting technical knowledge and solutions, leaders take an active role in supporting and enabling workers to adapt and make the changes required. They describe adaptive work as needed 'when our deeply held beliefs are challenged, when the values that made us successful become less relevant, and when legitimate yet competing perspectives emerge' (1997, p.6). In this place lies transformative work, as it requires deep and often more difficult change as it is linked to well established behaviours or beliefs which, as previously discussed, often form a part of our identity. Rather than a leader being the centre of change, adaptive leadership places this responsibility back with the collective group, requiring all people to make the changes required. Ronald Heifetz and Donald Laurie also note that leaders need to allow people to take initiative in defining and solving problems meaning that management supports rather than controls and workers step up to the responsibility (p.10). They comment that 'leadership has to take place everyday, it cannot be the responsibility of the few, a rarer event, or a once in a lifetime opportunity' (p.14). The responsibility to lead lies with all of us.

This concept of adaptive leadership again is well captured within the supervisor role. Supervisors understand that change can be difficult and that the responsibility for it lies with the worker. Rather than telling them they have to do it, they explore how and why it can be done and establish motivation for it to occur. This was nicely evidenced for me when someone I supervise was behind with a required administrative task. Their manager and I met with them and their manager pretty much said what the issue was, why they had to be done, and the consequences if they weren't. The worker and I went from this straight into supervision where with her permission I used motivational interviewing techniques along with identifying and challenging some deeply held beliefs around her reluctance toward required administrative tasks.

We then helped her explore and find ways to meet the named challenge and make the changes to adapt her work behaviour in this area. I could have just given her a list of things to try based on my own solutions but this wouldn't have worked. It was important she constructed and could then own what needed to happen. With the issue made clear by her manager it was our work that identified the adaptive processes required and how these would begin to be undertaken. As supervisors we need to tackle issues and not be afraid to help those we supervise face up to problems and adapt to changes in circumstances or required behaviour. Again, this type of naming is what good leaders do, as sheltering people from difficulties will often only delay the inevitable, nor does just prescribing what changes work either.

Leadership styles

If we accept that supervisors have a leadership function then it is important to identify styles of leadership that best support this. We have all experienced leadership styles in others that we have enjoyed and positively responded to, and those which create a lack of respect and immediate distancing or distrust. In his article on 'Leadership that gets results' Daniel Goleman (2000) talks about six different styles of leadership – coercive, authoritative, affiliative, democratic, pace setting, and coaching. He suggests that the more styles a leader exhibits the better, and effective leaders switch fluidly between the different styles of leadership, aware of how best to bring them into their leadership role. Coercive and pace setting styles both rely on the concept of 'do as I do' which is not what I think supervisors should be considering when applying leadership thinking into the supervisor role. Goleman suggests that leaders with a combination of authoritative, affiliative, democratic and coaching styles have the very best climate and business performance (p.87), and I will now focus on these four in more detail.

Authoritative leadership

Authoritative leadership encompasses an approach that mobilises people toward a vision, involves people in moving toward this by showing them how their work links to it, provides clear direction, is positive, and provides feedback about what is and isn't working in terms of achieving the bigger picture (Goleman 2000, pp.82–84). Autonomy to achieve tasks is provided so workers experience achievement and control in what they are undertaking but with a clear direction. There is room for innovation and to take calculated risks (Goleman 2000, p.84). Goleman cautions that an authoritative leadership style can become overbearing, or at times be dismissed. This is generally because workers are not on board with the vision due to perceiving the leader as not having enough knowledge or experience to support it.

Affiliative leadership

Affiliative leadership is people centred, empathic, creates harmony, and enhances relationships and communication. By enhancing relationships, trust is grown that supports sharing of ideas and innovation. This style of leadership generates a sense of commitment and of belonging (Goleman 2000, p.84). Again the caution is that this style of leadership can leave people a little directionless, and possibly does not provide enough feedback on poor performance. Goleman suggests that 'authoritative leaders state a vision, set standards, and let people know how their work is furthering the group's goals, alternate that with the caring, nurturing approach of the affiliative leader and you have a potent combination' (p.85).

Democratic leadership

A democratic style of leadership operates from principles of participation and collaboration and aims to achieve consensus through involvement in decision making. An immediate drawback can be frustration at endless meetings and a sense of a lack of direction and leadership (Goleman 2000, p.85).

Coaching style of leadership

A coaching style of leadership focuses on individual strengths and traits of workers and invests and grows these for the future. There tends to be a high level of delegating, established roles and responsibilities, and frequent dialogue about what is being achieved. It is perhaps the style that most exemplifies teaching and guiding. The drawback around the coaching style is the time it takes.

As supervisors I believe we engage aspects of these four styles of leadership in our role. We can see this in their core concepts, which can be summarised as:

- having a practice vision
- mobilising and motivating others
- being strongly positive
- showing empathy
- building relationships and communication
- getting consensus through participation

- identifying strengths and growing these
- overall enhancing work performance and development
- giving clear messages and feedback.

This is great summary of what supervisors can aspire to do, and in undertaking these tasks, they are hence taking a leadership role within the organisation. What is key is that a practice vision, or indeed vision of supervision, needs to align with wider organisational goals. If there is a disconnect here, say for example the organisation doesn't quite understand the role of supervision, supervisors need to step up to help educate those in positions of power about this. Given supervisors are often experienced practitioners, our practice vision and view of the direction of practice development needs to be heard. As said, supervisors are often quiet leaders and sometimes we need to turn up the volume on our practice voice and vision.

Leadership traits

The tasks of emotional intelligence as already discussed are what I believe to be the key to leadership and leadership within the supervisory role. Being self aware, able to manage and control our emotional responses, use this to increase our awareness of others and apply this knowledge to social contexts to especially support positive relationships, are fundamental in leadership. I heard an example of emotional intelligence missing in action from a manager who was telling a group of staff that their jobs were in scope for restructuring with possible serious implications – that is, job loss.

At some point in the meeting, a staff member sitting next to the manager reached over and touched them on the arm saying 'It must be hard for you, having to come in like this and tell people they might be losing their jobs'. The manager looked quite surprised and said brightly 'Oh no, not at all, I love change!' The meeting took a turn for the worse at about that moment. Respect, dignity, care, curiosity, openness, appreciation, courage, and vision are all components of good leadership. They are equally key components of good supervision.

Leaders need to have a strong sense of self and social responsibility whereby they are connected both to their own self and the wider social context. Through this awareness they can positively influence and inspire others to make change. As the 'eyes and ears' of practice, supervisors also have this potential to influence. Richard Barrett in his work on the seven levels of leadership consciousness identifies leadership traits as including calmness, focus, courage, responsibility, initiative, accountability, authenticity, integrity, passion, creativity, empathy, compassion and humility (2009b, p.2). Leaders need to be able to convey trust in others, evidenced by delegation, allowing workers to problem solve, and authority to work autonomously. Leaders should also be truthful and transparent, displaying fairness and giving explanations for decisions that are made. Effective leaders are prepared to source and identify new ideas that promote both their own and others' self actualisation (Barrett 2009b). I think leaders should be able to display humility and remain conscious of the authority they hold without over or under using this.

Transforming ourselves

By stepping up to the leadership potential within supervision, we take the opportunity to develop and challenge ourselves. Supervisors must stay engaged in a continuous and transformative learning process if this is expected of supervisees. The most obvious element of this is our use of our own supervision. With the supervisee's consent, it is essential we take issues to our supervisors that will extend our capacity, growth, and development. By deciding to include the task of practice leadership in our role we can examine and explore how well we are meeting. We can reflect on how well we challenged or explored practice, what we contributed to it in a session, and what the wider learning would be if it was taken out and given to a group of practitioners. We can imagine writing about what was discussed, explore what it taught us, what the gaps were and how changes to practice could support this.

As practice leaders, supervisors can identify patterns and trends in practice to be discussed and evaluated with other supervisors.

We can then take these further and highlight them to professional leaders or managers with suggestions on how practice could be advanced in these areas. We can take what has been gifted to us by a supervisee and make connection to it that benefits others through presenting and teaching. We can also support the practitioner to take the lead in offering their learning back through a presentation, teaching, writing, or leading a project around what they have discovered.

Susan Blumenfield and Irwin Epstein suggest that practitioners who are teaching must necessarily look at what they do critically and be responsive to the scrutiny and enquiry of others with differing perspectives (2001, p.8). The same applies to us as supervisors and this helps us critically reflect and examine our own clinical and supervisory practice. Through this, we develop practice based evidence, as mentioned in the introduction of this book, and the journey for it to become evidence based practice begins. Those that we work with hold so much knowledge and skill that is often kept only on a one to one level. The potential for this to contribute to wider change, if externalised and named, is very powerful, and should be modelled by us as supervisors.

In taking information outside of the session it is important to be respectful of the person and maintain confidentiality around their story. What you are sharing is the learning you have taken, not the detail of the supervisee's experience. This is exactly what should happen in supervision, our conversations should be less on the detail of an individual and family and more on the practitioner and their practice. It is the same for us, what we are sharing is our supervision practice and/or learning back to practice from what has been offered. This shows the reciprocity and mutuality that is evident in supervision as mentioned in the introduction of this book.

Another respectful and transformative way to do this is to share your personal and professional learning from what had been brought to supervision session with the supervisee and your reflection around it. I now always take a small amount of time toward the end of the session or during it, to offer my learning through these types of comments:

- 'Can I share something that I am taking away from our discussion today?'
- 'Something that occurred for me was...'
- 'Thank you for bringing this issue/topic today, it's really shown me...'
- 'What we've talked about today has really affirmed for me...'
- 'It's so interesting what you raised about... I'd really like to spend more time exploring that in my own thinking. Thank you...'

The key is to pay attention to the points of learning connection that you have made. It comes back to noticing our observations and what this might mean on a practice level in a wider context or for our own personal practice theory. It requires taking five or so minutes in the conclusion of the session to summarise your view and what you have taken from the person's work – this could be expressed through the use of language such as 'enhanced, reminded, curious about, really interested in'. My experience of doing this within or toward the end of a session is very positive. It helps create more of a 'levelling' and bringing in of equality. It suggests that we are journeying together around practice and it is always well received. My supervisees have almost appeared quite chuffed at times that I have taken something from the session, and it helps things end on a positive collegial note. It has now become essential to my supervision work, and helps me remain conscious and alert to their story and learning, and also my own.

Self reflection

We should be involved in a small formal reflection on a session each time we complete supervision with someone. The above process within the session contributes back to practice, while self reflection after a session contributes to our growth and development as supervisor in our supervisory practice. Margaret Morell suggests that supervisors can only improve and extend what they do if they are willing to make time before and after supervision sessions to prepare for and reflect on the sessions, and to consider, not only the material the supervisee has brought, but also, and more importantly, the supervisory processes taking place (2003, p.29).

I have already discussed earlier in the chapter on openness the need to become focused on the supervisee and centred into the session through the process of preparation and becoming open and attentive. I also agree that time taken after the session is extremely helpful to identify what went well and possibly not so well in my delivery of supervision.

For after the session, I have created a simple tool called the '5 Whats' which I mentally run through after I have provided supervision.

The '5 Whats'

1. What are my immediate thoughts and feelings when I reflect on the session? How would I rate it on a scale of zero to ten?

2. What went well in the session?

3. What could I have done differently?

4. What's my learning from the session?

5. What will I try to do more of/less of next time?

I ask myself these questions and because they draw from the Kolb learning cycle and solution focused questioning, find them a really helpful way to build learning from what I have done as a supervisor. The questions also help me to close off the session mentally, and transition into my next task. I also write up the notes straight away, which helps me reflect and either do the '5 Whats' before, during or after this process. Margaret Morrell comments that all supervisors regardless of experience should engage in this type of reflection after a supervision session (2003, p.29).

I had some conversations with experienced supervisors in social work at Wellington Hospital and asked them what they asked themselves in terms of reflection after a session? Here are some of their comments and thoughts:

- 'What's left with me, what feels unresolved?'
- 'Did I get too involved in the storyline?'
- 'It's hard not to be judgemental at times and jump in with advice, I need to stay aware of this, I wonder if we name that enough?'
- 'Was I supportive enough, was I helpful, did I do a good job?'
- 'That wasn't satisfying, what happened, why didn't I challenge the over focus on what seemed "safe"'?
- 'Did I provide a sounding board, a grounding place, was I supportive?'

I also asked them what they learned from providing supervision and they said the following:

- 'In what they bring…it gives me an appreciation of my own knowledge and skills.'
- 'It's exciting, it challenges me to hear better…it reminds me to be present and stay tuned in.'
- 'It increases my patience! I have to hold back, appreciate people, and sometimes get to the end in a different way.'
- 'I've realised people get their knowledge differently.'
- 'It's enriching of my professional and personal growth.'
- 'It's about finding your way through the story to the worker.'
- 'It contributes to a sense of my own competency and it meets an obligation to return what I have learnt. It's about being a part of a worker's journey.'
- 'Supervision is often the only place I get to hear about other people's work, it makes me feel I am part of a professional group.'
- 'Hearing about how someone approached a situation that may have frightened or scared me, gives me confidence to approach a situation like that… I take a deep breath and go into it taking them with me.'

I particularly like the last comment as this shows the reciprocity of learning that occurs in supervision, and that we too are always in a space of learning with the practitioners we are working with. Even experienced supervisors need to be involved in continuing education through attending training, workshops, reading and research not only in supervision but also around clinical practice. This helps us to remain connected to the areas of work that practitioners may practise in, along with honouring the process of supervision by continuing to up skill ourselves in it. This supports us to provide the best possible service not only to supervisees but those they work for. Involvement in projects, committees and attending conferences also helps us continue our education and professional development. At the end of any professional development opportunity that we participate in we can ask ourselves, 'What did I learn?' and 'How can I apply and contribute this learning to benefit others?'

Putting ourselves in the pathway of direct learning experiences should also include situations outside of both our supervisory and clinical practice. Taking the opportunity to engage in something quite different from our usual work helps stretch our minds to consider knowledge that we can call on in our supervisory practice. For example, this chapter centres on the notion of leadership, so putting ourselves in a leadership forum or learning context would be a great way to expand our thinking and delivery of our role.

The key to transformative learning is often about being bold and taking ourselves out of our comfort zones. Being with different professions, new topics, and giving ourselves exposure to different and new perspectives will all enhance our development and knowledge. It also means when the opportunity presents itself, we can take a risk and share a view or insight that may help bring about a transformative moment for a practitioner.

Conclusion

The chapter has explored the role of leadership within supervision and explored leadership styles, traits, and ways to give more voice to supervisors as practice leaders. The tasks of leadership align well to the personal and professional development aims of supervision. What is essential to this is demonstrating our own willingness to extend and grow our supervisor role through a process of reflection, awareness, insight, continuous learning and development. By putting ourselves in different learning contexts and embracing methods of self reflection we will contribute to provide a stimulating and meaningful learning experience for others. As leaders in practice, supervisors must step forward to contribute to not only practice change, but change in organisations and greater society. Through this we can strengthen ourselves to also challenge what may not be working well in our world, through growing in our leadership capacity and supporting this within others.

Conclusion

Whatever you can do, or dream, you can begin it.
Boldness has genius, power and magic in it.

Goethe (1749–1832)

This book has explored transformative supervision, describing it as shifts in thinking and behaviour that contribute to positive, long lasting change. Along with the normative, formative and supportive functions, the transformative function enables all of these to be taken in directions which support supervision as a place of powerful professional and personal development, always aimed at increasing the level of service we provide to others.

Supervision has been identified as a key place for transformative work to occur as it is often mandated by an organisation and offers a protected space from the noisy and busy nature of many workplaces. It provides a quiet place for reflection and development that deserves to be fully utilised. It can be seen as a 'base camp' which workers return to for replenishment and recuperation from the trials of the work they undertake. It needs to be well resourced and focused on equipping them to again go out to the demands of frontline practice. The opportunities supervision offers through allowing workers time to talk about their work and themselves within this are hugely valuable and need to be optimally taken advantage of. Supervisors need to see themselves as active participants in a worker's learning journey, and be prepared to take risks in questioning and applying new techniques to help support this.

Key to enabling the transformative function in supervision is the supervision relationship which should be built on a foundation of openness and honesty, providing a working partnership that models respect, care, empathy, careful use of humour, challenge and holistic recognition of the worker as a personal and professional being. This requires supervisors to tune into the world of the supervisee, and move beyond solely technical conversations to ones that explore emotional and intuitive reasoning. Supervisors need to apply their observations of these areas in creative ways that take both them and the supervisee into new places of exploration through a testing of hypotheses and ideas. Applying the transformative function in supervision helps workers and supervisors to become critical reflective and reflexive thinkers.

Supervisors need to remain mindful of the impact and influences of the environment that a practitioner is working within, and consider ways to help build resiliency and conscious awareness of this. The supervisor needs to consider the interaction of the worker's characteristics with those of their team, professional culture, and the organisation, and stay mindful of the global context which surrounds the work they are doing. Supervisors are required to be expansive and aware of these impacts and influences as a means of better supporting transformative moments that can also help manage burnout.

Supervision, while a place of solace and reflection, needs to remain mindful of the influence it can exert on creating positive change. To do this supervisors must see themselves as practice leaders and step up to bringing observations of practice and organisational impacts to the fore of leadership discussions. Supervisors need to be proactive in teaching, writing, and extending their practice knowledge to offer back the practice wisdom as both a supervisor and worker that they are accumulating. Leadership doesn't have to be reflected in a title or position, the fact that supervisors are in this role indicates confidence in their practice knowledge, and that they have something to offer others. Supervisors need to see themselves as catalysts of change both on individual worker and organisational levels. They need to take the responsibility that comes with this to ensure the supervision provided is dynamic and adaptable.

But why bother about lifting the transformative potential of supervision more to the fore? Well, the fundamental goal of life is to become self actualised beings, living out our full potential and individual truth. To do this we must place ourselves squarely in the pathway of learning. Dr David Bohm quoted in Joseph Jaworski's book says: 'Yourself is actually the whole of mankind… if you reach deeply into yourself, you are reaching deeply into the very essence of mankind. …we are all connected, if this could be taught, and if people could understand it, we would have a different consciousness' (1996, p.80). As human beings we do not operate in silos with no impact on each other, every one of us needs to recognise the interconnectedness that is a part of being human, and embrace these often relational connections as a way to discover more about ourselves.

Our earth is struggling to survive against the damage short term and selfish materialist gain thinking has inflicted upon it. No other species has wreaked such havoc on the world. We all have a role to play in changing this and this change must begin with ourselves. For those of us in human service work we need to take care in all of our interactions including those with the physical and ecological environment we are a part of. We must push back against the type of thinking that has allowed people to disconnect from the fact that we are all connected and dependent on everyone stepping up to undertake the changes required to help with the survival of our planet. To do this we must know ourselves and be continuously learning so our true selves are always present. We need to challenge thinking that reinforces difference and separateness and blocks our ability to be in true service with other people.

It is time to be bold in everything that we do. As supervisors we too need to step up and look at the work of supervision and see how we can take this to new levels to support personal and professional growth. We need to push back against supervision becoming another form of line management, or a way of managing risk adverse thinking that by nature squashes creative potential. Supervision is the place of development and learning and we need to be paying attention to when it is no longer achieving this. We need to become risk takers that try new methods and ideas to help lift learning to a whole new level that is exciting and rewarding. We too need to be continuously in a place of learning and development to help us grow and be of benefit to others.

A number of methods shared in this book draw from therapeutic techniques and as long as they remain linked to the work context, they are extremely useful in promoting transformative change and amplifying insight. We shouldn't fear using them because we worry that somehow they will turn us into therapists as they are proven ways of contributing to personal growth and change in every day ways, and to not use them is to deny their place within the supervision context. We need to keep growing our set of supervisory skills and adding new ideas and methods to this. This helps keeps supervision invigorating and innovative, for both supervisor and supervisee.

My experience of working in a transformative way in supervision has been hugely rewarding and exciting. I go into each supervision session on the look out for ways to connect the personal and professional selves and to take part in a journey of discovery with another person. The energy from working in this way is fantastic, and makes me feel that we have just embarked on a learning experience from which we have both gained. It is highly stimulating and conscious work that brings great insight to us both. Supervision becomes an event that is looked forward to and valued; it is sensitive and dynamic, challenging and affirming, and creative and responsive. It confirms my purpose and meaning in being a supervisor, and in who I am.

References

American Occupational Therapy Association (1999) 'Guide for supervision of occupational therapy personnel in the delivery of occupational therapy services.' *The American Journal of Occupational Therapy, 53,* 592–594.

Bar-On, R. (2005) *The Bar-On Model of Emotional Social intelligence (ESI).* Austin: University of Texas.

Barrett, R. (2009a) *The Seven Levels of Human Motivation.* Barrett Values Centre 2009. Available at www.valuescentre.com/uploads/2011-03-30/The%207%20 Levels%20of%20Human%20Motivation.pdf. Downloaded 15 January 2011.

Barrett, R. (2009b) *The Seven Levels of Leadership Consciousness.* Barrett Values Centre 2009. Available at www.valuescentre.com/uploads/2010-07-06/The%207%20 Levels%20of%20Leadership%20Consciousness.pdf. Downloaded 15 January 2011.

Beck, J. (1995) *Cognitive therapy. Basics and Beyond.* New York, NY: The Guilford Press.

Beddoe, L. (2010) 'Surveillance or reflection: Professional supervision in the "risk society."' *British Journal of Social Work, 40,* 4, 1279–1296.

Blumenfield, S. and Epstein, I. (2001) 'Promoting and maintaining a reflective professional staff in a hospital-based social work department.' *Social Work in Health Care, 33,* 3/4, 1–13.

Bohm, D. (1980) *Wholeness and the Implicate Order.* London: Routledge and Kegan Paul.

Bolte-Taylor, J. (2008) *My Stroke of Insight.* New York, NY: Penguin.

Bond, M. (2010) *In Depth Reflection – A Requirement for Supervision or Doing Your Head In?* Professional Supervision Conference: Common threads, different patterns. 29 April – 1 May 2010, Auckland, New Zealand.

Carifo, M.S. and Hess, A.K. (1987) 'Who is the ideal supervisor?' *Professional Psychology: Research and Practice, 18,* 244–250.

Carroll, M. and Tholstrup, M. (2001) *Integrative Approaches to Supervision.* London: Jessica Kingsley Publishers.

Carroll, M. (2005) 'Key issues in coaching psychology supervision.' *The Coaching Psychologist, 2,* 1, May 2006, 4–8.

Carroll, M. (2009) 'From mindless to mindful practice: On learning reflection in supervision.' *Psychotherapy in Australia, 15,* 4, 38–49.

Cherniss, C. and Equatios, E. (1997) 'Styles of clinical supervision in community mental health programs.' *Journal of Consulting and Clinical Psychology, 45,* 1195–1196.

Davis-Floyd, R. and Arvidson, P. S. (1997) *Intuition – the Inside Story. Interdisciplinary practices.* New York, NY: Routledge.

Davys, A. and Beddoe, L. (2010) *Best Practice in Professional Supervision: A Guide for the Helping Professions.* London: Jessica Kingsley Publishers.

De Shazer, S. (1988) *Clues: Investigating solutions in brief therapy.* New York, NY: W.W. Norton.

Dreyfus H.L. and Dreyfus S.E. (1986) *Mind over Machine: The Power of Human Intuition and Expertise in the Era of the Computer.* Oxford: Blackwell.

Durie, M. (1998) *Whai Ora: Maori Health Development.* Auckland: Oxford University Press.

Durie, M. (2009) *Global Transitions: Implications for a Regional Social Work Agenda.* Keynote speech, International Federation of Social Work (IFSW) Conference 2009, Auckland.

Encke, J. (2008) 'Breaking the Box: Supervision – A Challenge to Free Ourselves.' In R. Shohet (ed.) *Passionate Supervision.* London: Jessica Kingsley Publishers.

Eraut, M. (2005) 'Editorial: Expert and expertise, meanings and perspectives.' *Learning in Health and Social Care, 4,* 4, 173–179.

Exley, H. (1999) *Wisdom of the Millennium.* Watford and New York: Exley Publications.

Falender, C. and Shafranske, P. (2004) *Clinical Supervision: A Competency Based Approach.* Washington: American Psychological Association.

Fook, J. (2009) *Critical Reflection: Overview and Latest Ideas.* South West London Academic Network. Available at: www.aaswwe.asn.au/download/2009/conferslides/JanFookPresentationOverheads.ppt Downloaded 10 January 2011.

Fook, J., Ryan, M. and Hawkins, L. (2000) *Professional Expertise: Practice, Theory and Education for Working in Uncertainty.* London: Whiting and Birch.

Goleman, D. (2000) 'Leadership that gets results.' *Harvard Business Review March – April,* 78–9.

Goleman, D. (2004) *Emotional Intelligence: And Working with Emotional intelligence.* London: Bloomsbury.

Goleman, D. (2006) *Emotional Intelligence: Why it Can Matter more than IQ.* London: Bloomsbury.

Gray, I., Field, R., and Brown, K. (2010) *Effective Leadership, Management and Supervision in Health and Social Care.* Exeter: Learning Matters Ltd.

Guest, P.D. and Beutler, L.E. (1988) 'Impact of psychotherapy supervision on therapist orientation and values.' *Journal of Consulting and Clinical Psychology, 56,* 653–658.

Heath, P. and Crotty, E. (2010) *Creative Expression in Supervising Practice.* A workshop in Professional Supervision Conference: Common threads, different patterns. 29 April – 1 May 2010, Auckland, New Zealand.

Heifetz, R.A. and Laurie, D.L. (1997) 'The work of leadership.' *Harvard Business Review, 75,* 1, 124–134.

Herkt, J., and Hocking, C. (2007) 'Supervision in New Zealand: Professional growth or maintaining competence?' *New Zealand Journal of Occupational Therapy, 54,* 2, 24–30.

Howe, D. (2008) *The Emotionally Intelligent Social Worker.* New York, NY: Palgrave Macmillan.

Horwath, J., and Morrison, T. (2007) 'Collaboration, integration and change in children's services: Critical issues and key ingredients.' *Child Abuse and Neglect, 31,* 1, 55–69.

Jackson, A. and Segal, S. (2002) *Social Work Health and Mental Health: Practice, Research and Programs.* New York, NY: The Haworth Social Work Practice Press.

Jaworski, J. (1996) *Synchronicity – The Inner Path of Leadership.* San Francisco, CA: Berrrett-Koehler Publishers Inc.

Kavanagh, C.K. (2002) 'Good fences don't necessarily make good therapists'. *Annals of the American Psychotherapy Association, 5,* 34.

Kolb, D. (1984) *Experiential learning.* Englewood cliffs, NJ: Prentice Hall.

Kübler-Ross, E. (1986) *Death: The Final Stage of Growth.* New York, NY: Simon and Schuster/Touchstone.

Lorenz, E. (1972) 'Predictability: Does a butterfly flapping its wings in Brazil set off a tornado in Texas?' Available at http://voluntaryboundaries.blogsome.com/category/edward-n-lorenz/ accessed 20 June 2011.

Luft, J., and Ingham, H. (1955) 'The Johari Window, a Graphic Model of Interpersonal Awareness.' In the *Proceedings of the Western Training Laboratory in Group Development.* Los Angeles, CA: UCLA.

Maidment, J. (2006) 'The quiet remedy: A dialogue on reshaping professional relationships.' *Families in Society, 87,* 1, 115–121.

Miller, W. and Moyers, T. (2006) 'Eight stages in learning motivational interviewing.' *Journal of Teaching in the Addictions, 5,* 1, 3–14.

Miller, W. and Rollnick, S. (2002) *Motivational Interviewing: Preparing People for Change.* New York, NY: Guilford Press.

Ministry of Health (2000) *The New Zealand Health Strategy.* Wellington, New Zealand: Ministry of Health.

Morrell, M. (2003) 'Forethought and afterthought: Two of the keys to professional development and good practice in supervision.' *Social Work Review, Autumn/Winter 2003,* 29–32.

Morrison, T. (1993) *Staff Supervision in Social Care.* Essex: Longman Information and Reference.

Morrison, T. (1997) 'Emotionally competent child protection organisations: fallacy, fiction or necessity?.' In J Bates, R. Pugh and N. Thompson (Eds.) *Protecting Children: Challenges and Changes.* Arena: Aldershot.

Morrison, T. (2007) 'Emotional intelligence, emotion and social work: Context, characteristics, complications and contributions.' *British Journal of Social Work 37,* 2, 245–263.

Munford, R. and Sanders, J. (2010) 'Embracing the diversity of practice: Indigenous knowledge and mainstream social work practice.' *Journal of Social Work Practice, 25,* 1, 63–77.

Munro, E. (2008) 'Improving reasoning in supervision.' *Social Work Now: The Practice Journal of Child, Youth and Family, 40,* 3–10.

O'Connell, B., and Jones, C. (1997) 'Solution focused supervision.' *Counselling* November, 289–292.

O'Donoghue, K. (1998) *Supervising Social Workers: A Practical Handbook.* Palmerston North: School of Policy Studies and Social Work, Massey University.

O'Donoghue, K. (2003) *Re-storying Social Work Supervision.* Palmerston North, New Zealand: Dunmore Press Ltd.

Opie, A. (2000) *Thinking Teams/Thinking Clients.* New York, NY: Columbia University Press.

Parton, N. (2008) 'Changes in the form of knowledge in social work: From the "social" to the "informational".' *British Journal of Social Work, 38,* 253–268.

Payne, M. (1997) *Modern Social Work Theory* (2nd edition) Hampshire: Macmillan Press Ltd.

Payne, M. (2008) 'Complexity and social work theory and practice.' *Social Work Now: The Practice Journal of Child, Youth and Family, 39,* 15–20.

Peck, M.S. (1990) *The Road Less Travelled.* London: Arrow Books, Random House.

Perry, B. (1997) 'Incubated in Terror: Neurodevelopment Factors in the 'Cycle of Violence'.' In J. Osofsky (ed.) *Children, Youth and Violence: The Search for Solutions.* New York, NY: Guilford Press.

Pithouse, A. (1987) *Social Work: The Organisation of an Invisible Trade.* London: Gower.

Profitt, N.J. (2008) 'Who cares about us? Opening paths to a critical collective notion of self-care.' *Canadian Social Work Review, 25,* 2, 146–167.

Polanyi, M. (2009) *The Tacit Dimension.* Chicago, IL: University of Chicago Press.

Reder, P., Duncan, S. and Gray, M. (1993) *Beyond Blame.* London: Routledge.

Royal- Tanaere, A. (1997) 'Maori human development learning theory.' In *Mai I. Rangiatea P. Te Whaiti,* (eds), P. McCarthy and A. Durie. Auckland, New Zealand: Auckland University Press.

Ruch, G., Turney, D., and Ward, A. (2010) *Relationship Based Social Work: Getting to the Heart of Practice.* London: Jessica Kingsley Publishers.

Salovey, P. and Mayer, J. (1990) 'Emotional intelligence.' *Imagination, Cognition and Personality, 9,* 3, 185–211.

Serge, P.M. (1990) The Fifth Discipline. *The Art and Science of the Learning Organisation.* New York, NY: Doubleday cuurency.

Senge, P.M. (2008) 'The Power of Presence.' 2-CD set. Colorado, CO: Sounds True.

Senge, P., Scharmer, O.C., Jaworski, J., and Flowers, B.S. (2005) *Presence: Exploring Profound Change in People, Organisations and Society.* London: Nicholas Brealey Publishing.

SETA (Society of Eastern Thought and Awareness) 'Knowledge of Reality' magazine edition 18 'Gut feelings.' Available at www.sol.com.au/kor/kor_18.htm. Downloaded 4 January 2011.

Sheppard, M. (2007) 'Assessment: From Reflexivity to Process Knowledge.' In J. Lishman (ed.) *Handbook for Practice Learning in Social Work and Social Care: Knowledge and Theory.* London: Jessica Kingsley Publishers.

Shohet, R. (ed.) (2008) *Passionate Supervision.* London: Jessica Kingsley Publishers.

Siebert, A. (2006) 'Strengthening workforce resiliency in the public sector.' *The Public Manager,* Autumn, 3–7.

Siebert, D.C. (2005) 'Personal and occupational factors in burnout among practicing social workers: Implications for researchers, practitioners, and managers.' *Journal of Social Service Research, 32,* 2, 25–44.

Sinetar, M. (1986) *Ordinary People as Monks and Mystics: Lifestyles for Self Discovery.* New Jersey, NJ: Paulist Press.

Smith, M. (2000) 'Supervision of fear in social work: A re-evaluation of reassurance.' *Journal of Social Work Practice 14,* 1, 17–26.

St Luke's Innovative Resources. (2001) *Strength to strength course materials.* Bendigo, Australia: St Luke's.

Sveiby, K. (1997) 'Tacit knowledge.' Available at www.sveiby.com/www.sveiby.com/articles/Polanyi, accessed 23 June 2011.

Teilhard de Chardin, P. (1959) *The Phenomenon of Man.* London: Williams Collins Sons and Co Ltd. and New York, NY: Harper and Brothers. (Translation, original French 1955.)

Thiele, L. (2006) *The Heart of Judgement; Practical Wisdom, Neuroscience and Narrative.* Cambridge: Cambridge University Press.

Thorpe, K. (2004) 'Reflective learning journals: from concept to practice.' *Reflective Practice, 5,* 3, 327–343.

Tolle, E. (1999) *The Power of Now. A Guide to Spiritual Enlightenment.* Sydney: Hodder Headline Australia Pty Ltd.

Tolle, E. (2005) *A New Earth: Awakening to Your Life's Purpose.* United States: Penguin Publishing.

Tuckman, Bruce W. (1965) 'Developmental sequence in small groups.' *Psychological Bulletin 63,* 384–399. The article was reprinted in *Group Facilitation: A Research and Applications Journal,* Number 3, Spring 2001.

Turnell, A. and Edwards, S. (1999) *Signs of Safety: A Solution and Safety Orientated Approach to Child Protection Casework.* New York, NY: W.W. Norton and Co.

Wakefield, J. and Baer, J. (2008) 'Levels of meaning and the case for theoretical integration.' *Social Work Now: The Practice Journal of Child, Youth and Family, 39,* 21–28.

Walsh, F. (2008) 'Using theory to support a family resilience framework in practice.' *Social Work Now. The Practice Journal of Child, Youth and Family, 39,* 5–14.

Weld, N. (2006) 'Awareness and emotions.' *Social Work Now: The Practice Journal of Child, Youth and Family, New Zealand, 35,* 4–7, December.

Weld, N. (2009) 'Making sure children get 'HELD' – Ideas and resources to help workers place Hope, Empathy, Love, and Dignity at the heart of child protection and support.' Dorset: Russell House Publishing.

Weld, N. and Appleton, C. (2008) *Walking in People's Worlds: A Practical and Philosophical Approach to Social Work.* Auckland, New Zealand: Pearson Education.

Wexler, J. (2010) *Supervision and State of Being.* Professional Supervision Conference: Common threads, different patterns. 29 April – 1 May 2010, Auckland, New Zealand.

White, M. and Epston, D. (1990) *Narrative Means to Therapeutic Ends.* New York, NY: W.W Norton.

Zaleznik, A. (1977) 'Managers and Leaders: Are they different?' *Harvard Business Review,* May–June, 67–78.

Subject Index

Author Index